Great Issues of the Day
ISSN 0270-7947
Number Two

THE TRILEMMA OF
WORLD OIL POLITICS

by
Sheikh R. Ali and Jeffrey M. Elliot
North Carolina Central University

*Edited by Paul David Seldis
and Michael Burgess*

R. REGINALD
The Borgo Press
San Bernardino, California □ MCMXCI

10/92

10323084

THE BORGO PRESS
Publishers Since 1975
Post Office Box 2845
San Bernardino, CA 92406
United States of America

*   *   *   *   *   *   *   *

Library of Congress Cataloging-in-Publication Data

Ali, Sheikh Rustum.
  The trilemma of world oil politics / by Sheikh R. Ali and Jeffrey M. El-
liot ; edited by Paul David Seldis and Michael Burgess.
    p. cm. — (Great issues of the day, ISSN 0270-7497 ; no. 2)
  Bibliography: p.
  Includes index.
  ISBN 0-89370-168-8. — ISBN 0-89370-268-4 (pbk.)
  1. Petroleum industry and trade—Political aspects—Arab countries. 2.
Petroleum industry and trade—Political aspects—United States. 3. United
States—Foreign relations—Near East. 4. Near East—Foreign relations—
United States. 5. World politics—1945- . I. Elliot, Jeffrey M. II. Title.
III. Series.
HD9578.A55A5485 1991   84-275
327.1'11—dc19   CIP

FIRST EDITION

CONTENTS

INTRODUCTION

Of all the industries in the world, oil leads in volume and monetary value. It is the one industry that interests every country in the world, affecting the life styles of almost every living being to one degree or another. Oil has revolutionized civilization and continues to provide the energy to sustain it. Almost daily the world media concern themselves with the price and availability of oil. Why?

There are many reasons: much of the oil trade moves through international channels; high profits are made by oil companies; the oil industry itself is vital to both producing and consuming nations alike; oil imports affect the balance of payments of both developed and developing nations; oil is such a vital necessity that the lack of it could paralyze modern civilization.

As a result of its importance, oil lies at the root of many international, political, and economic disagreements, affecting companies, governments, organizations, and individuals alike. It is a commodity like no other, and despite its current price depreciation, remains paramount as an eco-political industry, as well as a strategic weapon.

This book presents a worldwide view of past, present, and potential uses of oil as a political instrument. It examines the eternal tripartite conflict between the oil-producing countries, companies, and consumers. Oil needs and problems are ubiquitous, permeating all political realities, but subject also to economic constraints, resource allocations, and potential technological breakthroughs, further complicated by the massive environmental impact caused by oil development.

Today's continuing world energy crisis was triggered, but not caused by, the Arab-Israeli War of 1973, and the resultant oil embargo imposed by the Arab states. The geometric growth in demand for energy among the developed industrial nations had drawn far too little attention from economists and politicians alike, as finite supplies of the popular energy source were steadily consumed.

The energy crisis unexpectedly burst upon the political scene, as America and other industrialized nations suddenly faced shortages and price increases. America's preeminent position in the world was being challenged by the rising power of the Arab nations. With the formation of the Organization of Arab Petroleum Exporting Countries (OAPEC) in 1968, a new power center emerged, one whose stated purpose was to reduce the power of Western oil companies, and to control their own oil resources.

OAPEC was formed outside of its parent body—the Organization of Petroleum Exporting Countries (OPEC)—because the Arab sheikhs believed that "where there are Arabs there is oil." Indeed, the world's largest oil reserves are centered in or around the Arabian Peninsula. OAPEC, like OPEC, is an organization bent toward the correction of perceived past injustices. The founders of OPEC and OAPEC understand perfectly well that the world cannot do without their oil.

This study reveals a pattern in the control of Middle Eastern oil correlating to the international relations of the day. Thus, when Great Britain relinquished its role as the manager of international relations by the middle of the twentieth century, the United States assumed the responsibility, and hence the dominance, of Arab oil, only to find itself contending with the rising power of the Soviet Union and the growing independence of the Arab nations.

The increasing demand for oil in all countries has caused it to become the most vital source of energy in the world. International oil is a multibillion dollar industry that affects, in varying degrees, the balance of payments between the oil-exporting and oil-consuming nations.

As the least expensive and most abundant oil supplies have become concentrated in the Middle East, the industrialized world has, in turn, become increasingly dependent on the whims of Arab leaders. In 1973, when the Arabs implemented their threat to reduce oil production and imposed an embargo on oil supplies to the world, they also stepped up diplomatic efforts to force Israel to withdraw from occupied Arab lands. Since then, the Middle East has continued to be the center of strife among the powers of the world, be they small or large. The recent Iraqi invasion of Kuwait and the resulting Gulf War between an international coalition headed by the United States and Iraq further illustrates that the Middle East has become the Balkan flashpoint of late twentieth-century geopolitics.

This book further focuses on the effectiveness of the Arab "oil weapon" to accomplish its defined aims; and it examines the extent to which the Arabs can expect future successes. It also considers the real possibility of another Arab oil embargo in the event of a renewed Arab-Israeli war. The impact of such an embargo on the Western and Japanese economies would be devastating. Clearly, the United States—or a coalition of Western nations led by the United States—would be forced to respond with military, political, and economic action to prevent the economic strangulation of the industrialized Western world. The options, limitations, and conditions surrounding the use of oil as an instrument of Arab interests are thoroughly analyzed in the following pages.

America's dependence on overseas oil cannot be eliminated in the foreseeable future, except at what would seem to be prohibitive cost. What is needed, among other things, is some overall taxonomy of energy: a listing of options and priorities, so that national debate will lead to public illumination and, eventually, to satisfactory policy decisions. Unfortunately, the current oil glut has lulled the American public into believing the crisis is over. It most emphatically is not. The question remains: how can the United States maintain its oil reserves in the face of ever-dwindling supplies and threatened harsh OPEC demands? This study investigates the answers and possible alternatives to such questions.

The trilemma of world oil politics—that is, the conflicting and, in some ways, contrasting, interests of the oil-producing and oil-consuming countries with the multinational oil companies—has garnered considerable attention in the last twenty years. The most powerful and least vulnerable country among them, the

United States, has become increasingly alarmed at the prospect of relying on ever-larger quantities of oil (mostly from the Middle East) as its primary energy source. Japan depends upon Arab oil for approximately eighty percent of its energy needs; so, to a lesser extent, does Western Europe. Middle Eastern oil is a vital necessity for the continued progress and even survival of the industrialized world as we know it.

It is easily conceivable that oil superpower Saudi Arabia may fall into the hands of Arab radicals and Muslim hardliners, thereby toppling the traditional monarchy. Beset by threats from within and without, the Saudis, America's staunchest supplier of oil, show increasing signs that the monarchy's days are numbered. How long can the world, and particularly the energy-hungry Western world, depend upon such a precarious situation?

The Soviet Union, bolstered by its considerable internal oil supply, has long supported oil price increases. The emerging influence of the Soviet Union among the oil producing and -exporting nations (PEN), coupled with the marked decline of American influence in most of those countries, continues to threaten the consistent supply of energy to Western countries.

During the Arab oil embargo in 1973-74, the Soviet Union sought to maximize its gains via the weakening of Western economies and the resultant strains imposed on the capitalist world. The Soviets maintained a public posture as a "friend" and ally to the Arabs in their military efforts against Israel, and hoped to benefit by the Arab nations' struggle against the Western oil monopolies.

The USSR's own oil resources have fluctuated throughout the years. However, for the moment, it appears that the Soviet Union will continue to be one of the world's largest producers of oil and a net exporter. Soviet influence in the Arab world, especially in Algeria, Iraq, Libya, Syria, and Yemen, remains strong. Revolution remains a potent possibility in the conservative Arab states, and the Soviet Union can be expected to exploit any instability that might develop.

In a world where the price and availability of oil are critically important to many nations, the emergence of the People's Republic of China as an oil-producing and -exporting country is a welcome sign. However, the over-enthusiastic reports of record-breaking oil discoveries there remain unrealistic; those familiar with Chinese estimates know that such approximations are nothing more than hopeful targets. At present, the Chinese and Soviets play a relatively minuscule role in the world's oil trade. The USSR does, however, exert a greater influence in manipulating the world's oil supply.

The world energy crisis is symptomatic of the failure of the international political system. Oil is the most international of all the world's problems. The two superpowers, the industrialized nations of both Western and Eastern Europe, Japan, as well as the pre-industrialized and non-industrialized countries of the Third World, are all interested in securing long-term oil supplies at reasonable prices. The oil producers are aware that their drive for higher prices evokes little sympathy among those nations who must ultimately pay for such increases. Subsequently, a tremendous economic disparity between the oil-haves and have-nots has taken place. In the wake of this fluctuating economic chaos two kinds of interlocking diplomacies are emerging: resource diplomacy and basket diplomacy. The concept of the former is evolving as a result of a seemingly limitless demand on critical resources, and attempts by the industrialized states to control these resources. The latter is an attempt, in those nations which are victims of their own resource constraints, to turn begging hands into productive hands. These nations are relying to a great degree on foreign aid to help fill the gap between survival and reaching a point of economic no return. Unfortunately, this policy has in many cases resulted in such nations accruing enormous debts that are essentially unpayable, and that spell potential economic disaster for the future.

As nations struggle to maintain themselves, there is a strong possibility that resource diplomacy and basket diplomacy will be major factors in the world arena in the decades ahead, either by forging cooperation between the rich and poor nations, or between the established members of the industrialized world and the nouveau riche oil nations on the one hand, and the resourceless poor countries on the other.

Finally, a few words on methodology. We have employed descriptive analysis, with a major emphasis on empirical data and documentary evidence, to focus on both the political and economic aspects of world oil politics. The book occasionally draws from Dr. Ali's earlier work, *Saudi Arabia and Oil Diplomacy* (Praeger, 1976).

—Dr. Sheikh R. Ali
Dr. Jeffrey M. Elliot
North Carolina Central University
August, 1991

I.

THE POLITICS OF OIL

Perceptions of oil supply, demand, and price have changed over the last twenty years on an almost continuous basis. The 1973-74 Arab oil embargo, the 1978-79 interruption in Iranian exports, and the subsequent war between Iraq and Iran, are all periods for which inventory levels are cited as explanations why oil supply shortages were more serious than might have been expected.

A new outlook has emerged in the 1990s. Many observers believe that, barring major accidents or incidents, oil supply-and-demand balance will remain slack for the future, and that world demand for oil is shrinking. To be sure, say the pundits, oil is still king, but the nature of its power is changing. Oil has ceased to assert itself as a force merely through its availability; it still holds sway, however, through pricing levels. The high prices of the 1970s and early 1980s forced users to conserve energy and to develop other sources of fuel; this, combined with world economic recession, resulted in the world oil price collapse of 1986.

Three factors explain the politics of oil supply, demand, and price: location, production, and consumption. In order to understand the intricate relationship between these factors and the bargaining process that has evolved between producers and consumers, we must first understand the history of the oil industry.

The expansion of the petroleum trade in both the nineteenth century and in the early twentieth century was soundly based on the efforts of many nations to raise their standard of living. The growing indispensability of oil to the industrial world made its availability imperative. Mounting demand simultaneously made its production and distribution an attractive commercial proposition.

It took World War I to transform "oil from being a source of revenue for tycoons and speculators into a vital industrial and strategic material."[1] For half a century, oil had illuminated the world; it was now powering the machines of war—the tanks, planes, trucks, and even the taxies that enabled armies to fight were all propelled by gasoline. Petroleum became equally important to the world's navies as admirals realized its advantage over coal.

When World War I broke out in 1914, the world's two major oil producers were the United States and Tsarist Russia. Some petroleum products were also exported by Indonesia, Romania, and Mexico. On the eve of the war, oil had just been discovered in commercial quantities in Venezuela; as the war progressed, however, Russian oil faded from the world picture.

In contrast to the United States, with its ample domestic reserves, Great Britain had to depend completely upon foreign sources for its petroleum. Consequently, the British government gave direct diplomatic and military support to William Knox D'Arcy in his pioneering oil venture in Iran, and even became part owner of the Anglo-Persian Oil Company.

During this period, oil exploration and exports were focused primarily on the most promising areas, such as the United States, the Caribbean, the Middle East, and Indonesia. Europe and Africa were regarded with little interest.

When World War I concluded, the struggle for control of Middle Eastern oil fields ended with the formation of a cartel by the seven major oil companies, also known as the "seven sisters": Standard Oil Company of New Jersey, Standard Oil Company of California, Socony-Vacuum Oil Company, Gulf Oil Corporation, the Texas Company, Royal Dutch-Shell Oil Company, and British Petroleum. To this list can be added an eighth, Compagnie Française des Petroles. The attempts by these companies to establish a monopoly, or rather an oligopoly, over the production, refining, and marketing of oil was aimed at establishing a means of regulating price and competition in order to guarantee maximum profits to all its members.

At the end of the World War I, Royal Dutch-Shell was producing 84,000 barrels per day, compared to New Jersey Standard's 27,000. The two companies had a virtual monopoly in Egypt, Venezuela, and British Borneo, as well as controlling ninety-six percent of production in the Dutch East Indies, and eleven percent in the Soviet Union.[2] From 1922 onwards, the United States produced more oil than its refineries could handle, and the refineries generated more product than the market could absorb.[3] Important, too, were the new discoveries in Venezuela. From two million barrels in 1922, Venezuela's production rose to nine million barrels in 1924 and to 106 million in 1928, when it replaced the Soviet Union as the world's second largest oil producer.[4] In 1930, vast oil fields were discovered in Texas, causing prices to drop quickly from $1.30 a barrel to five cents a barrel.[5]

Oil was discovered in several Middle East countries during the 1930s, but the total production of the region in 1938 amounted to only some fifteen million tons [See Table 1].

During World War II, the need for petroleum and petroleum-related products reached monumental proportions. Allied strategy centered around efforts to interrupt or even terminate Germany's oil supply, all of which had to be imported. Without a doubt, such actions were vital to allied efforts to secure a victory.

TABLE I

The Main Oil-Producing Countries, 1938

Country	Million Tons
United States	161.9
Venezuela	27.9
Iran	10.2
Mexico	5.5
Iraq	4.4

Source: Christopher Tugendhat. *Oil: The Biggest Business.* New York: G. P. Putnam's Sons, 1968.

The Turning Point

Toward the end of the 1940s, the United States became a net importer of oil. The result was the coupling of low-cost Middle Eastern oil with the high prices of American petroleum, thus giving the major oil companies a magnitude of profit which allowed them to invest in large-scale downstream facilities. The major effect of the decolonization of the Afro-Asian countries, and the creation of the United Nations with its atmosphere of "one state, one vote" on the oil industry, was to change the rules of the game. This started a round of discussions between the cartel and their host countries, which ultimately culminated in a 50/50 profit-sharing formula. The first change in this system occurred in Venezuela in 1943:

> Originally, the rulers and governments of these countries got some modest initial payments on granting a concession, usually combined with some rental for the territory covered by the concessions: thereafter, if oil was found in quantities which justified exploitation, amounts varying with the quantity of oil, i.e., a so-called royalty, became payable too.[6]

In 1950, Saudi Arabia became the first Middle Eastern nation to implement the 50/50 split, and by 1952 all other of the region's significant producers had followed suit, with the exception of Iran. Although the agreement between King Abd al-Aziz ibn Saud and Aramco (the American Arabian Oil Company) gave the Saudi government half the profits earned by crude oil production, it also limited the Saudi government's right to impose higher taxes, thus putting it in a less favorable position than the Venezuelan government.

As a result of the large-scale relinquishment of acreage by the major oil companies, a proliferation of new agreements emerged from the growing chaos. These new arrangements were mainly between various national oil companies of the producing countries, which were viewed by the host countries as symbols of their national aspirations to gain a place in the sun,[7] and either the established (or new) companies of the industrialized world, and/or the consuming governments themselves. The newcomers included several American independents, plus various newly established consuming-country national companies. The new agreements took the form of equity participation, risk-taking, and vertical integration, among others:

> Both the major companies and the newcomers were successful at finding oil beyond their wildest dreams. In the late 1940s when the newcomers began to appear on the international scene, there were still lingering fears that one of the problems of the postwar world would be a shortage of oil, and reserves were sufficient to last for less then fifteen years at the prevailing rate of production. By 1960, there was enough to last for over forty years, despite the vast increase in consumption, and the industry's main problem was to find ways of preventing the flood of new discoveries from wreckage of price wars.[8]

TABLE 2

Oil Production by Main Areas, 1946-51
(Millions of Tons)

Year	U.S.	Caribbean	Mid East	USSR	World
1946	244	62	35	23	385
1947	262	69	42	27	424
1948	290	77	57	30	483
1949	267	76	70	34	482
1950	283	86	87	37	535
1951	322	97	96	42	608

Source: British Petroleum Co., *Statistical Review of the World Oil Industry*. London: British Petroleum, 1956.

World crude oil supplies were boosted by discoveries of major new supply sources [See Table 2]. From the mid-1950s to the early-1960s international oil was a steadily increasing surplus with a simultaneously declining price structure. The causes for this paradox were both commercial and political.

Concerning the former, Christopher Tugendhat states:

> The industry is not a monolithic whole; it is a collection of

different companies with conflicting interests which have to compete with each other in order to earn their profits. Some...have more oil than they need. But this is no consolation for Shell...nor for the Italian ENI and French ERAP. For these groups, the fact that there is a world surplus of oil is quite immaterial. It belongs to other people, and they want their own. Not even the reserve-rich companies can afford to rest on their laurels....As the key to profitability in the international oil industry is to have a source of supply as close as possible to every market.[9]

This political paradox derives from the fact that the Middle East is blessed with seventy-five percent of the world's oil reserves and forty-six percent of production.[10] Six of the world's ten leading oil-producing countries in 1968 had virtually no recorded output in 1925. Many of the larger Middle Eastern oil discoveries date from the late 1930s or after. The impact of these vast new oil supplies after World War II established a new set of fuel patterns and promoted widespread changes in the industrialized world.

The increase in oil output in the post-war years was made possible by the discovery of huge oil reserves in the 1930s, and by a simultaneous increase in demand from Europe, Japan, the United States, and other consuming countries. The large margin between receipts and outlays may be attributed in part to the exceedingly low costs of the raw product, and also to the disparity in payments to local governments, which continued through 1950 to be made mainly on a fixed royalty basis. Even when profit-sharing agreements were concluded, in most of these countries the real amounts received by the governments, although increased, were offset by a slow rise in oil prices, and greatly reduced the producing governments' actual share of petroleum revenue.

To comprehend further the problem of oil supply and demand on a global basis, the balance between production and consumption in various countries must be considered. The countries which produce more than they consume must act as a source of supply for the countries which produce less.

In the 1960s, some producing countries, notably the United States and the Soviet Union, were both exporters and importers of oil. During this period, when American production exceeded its domestic consumption, the Caribbean was a major source of supply for Eastern Hemisphere oil requirements. Most of the Caribbean production came from Venezuela, which was second only to the United States in annual production. Although production had continued to rise, by the 1980s the Western Hemisphere as a whole did not produce enough oil to meet its own energy requirements.

Large, proven oil reserves are concentrated in very few areas, most notably in the Middle East. Therefore, the Western Hemisphere must look increasingly to this region to make up its own domestic deficits in oil production. Japan and Europe are even more dependent upon the Middle East than is the United States. Some of the gap is made up by other areas: Indonesia contains several rich oil properties, and is now a substantial exporter. Similarly, a series of major petroleum discoveries in North Africa and Nigeria indicate that these countries are destined to become important exporters of crude oil, particularly to the nearby markets of Western Europe.

Oil prices increased steadily during World War II, then plummeted at war's end. During the 1950s, the oil majors were successful in avoiding any sharp changes in prices. With increased supplies of oil from North Africa and a rise in exports from the Soviet Union, the oil cartel reduced the posted price of oil in 1959 by eighteen cents, and again in 1960 by ten cents.

The petroleum pricing structure of the 1950s "was a logical method for pricing oil in world markets under the supply conditions and industrial structure prevailing prior to the Second World War."[11] The system of posted prices, at which the companies stood ready to purchase crude at the wellhead, was tied to the income of the producing countries. Consequently, the oil cartel maintained posted crude prices, but compensated for their losses by juggling their books to show downstream losses in the consuming countries. The consuming countries resented both the ensuing loss of fiscal revenue, and the fact that they were not being compensated with a reduction in the foreign exchange cost of their oil imports. Acceding to stiff pressure from the West, the oil companies were forced to reduce their posted prices for crude. While the reductions were not large, their impact was a shock to the oil producing countries, and in reaction they formed their own cartel in 1960—the Organization of Petroleum Exporting Countries (OPEC). OPEC was successful in preventing further reductions in oil prices, which remained virtually steady for the ensuing decade.

After years of bargaining between OPEC and the oil companies, the system of posted prices was transformed into a "tax reference" system that, for all intents and purposes, could not be unilaterally reduced by the petroleum industry. A formula for royalties was also reached which gave a larger share of profits to the producing countries. They were able to change the concession patterns by directly bargaining with the oil companies, and not going through the auspices of OPEC. An important aspect of this achievement was the large-scale relinquishment or confiscation of acreage held by the oil industry, giving the oil producing nations a source of additional revenue and also enhancing their bargaining power.

> It could be argued that all OPEC achieved had been on behalf of its Middle East members, not the others. Alternatively, you could rationalize it a little sourly by saying that anything which increased the tax-paid cost of Middle East oil helped Venezuela by making its oil to some extent more competitive.[12]

As a result of the 1967 Arab-Israeli War, the resulting Arab oil embargo and the closing of the Suez Canal, oil shipments from North Africa to Western countries increased to fill the gap. Europe became more dependent on Libya as the civil war in Nigeria and the disruption of the Trans-Arabian Pipeline by Syria decreased oil supplies from Nigeria and Saudi Arabia. Libya was now supplying about thirty percent of Europe's oil needs.[13]

TABLE 3

Oil Production Capacity, 1985-1995
(Millions of barrels per day)

Country/Region	1985 (est.)	1990 (proj.)	1995 (proj.)
Non-OPEC			
United States	11.2	9.9-10.4	8.3-9.3
Canada	1.8	1.8-2.0	1.8-2.3
Mexico	3.2	3.2-3.5	3.5-4.0
North Sea	3.9	3.6-4.0	3.3-3.9
Other Non-OPEC	7.1	7.1-7.7	6.5-7.5
Total Non-OPEC	27.2	26.1-27.1	24.3-25.9
OPEC			
Algeria	1.2	0.8-1.2	0.6-0.9
Ecuador	0.3	0.2-0.3	0.1-0.2
Gabon	0.2	0.1-0.2	0.1-0.2
Indonesia	1.7	1.4-1.6	1.2-1.4
Iran	3.2	2.5-3.5	2.5-3.5
Iraq	1.3	2.5-3.5	4.0-5.0
Kuwait	1.6	1.6-1.8	1.7-2.0
Libya	1.8	1.8-2.2	1.8-2.2
Nigeria	2.2	1.9-2.1	1.6-2.0
Qatar	0.6	0.5-0.7	0.4-0.6
Saudi Arabia	9.2	9.2-10.2	9.2-11.2
UAE	1.6	1.6-2.0	2.0-2.2
Venezuela	2.4	2.0-2.4	1.8-2.2
Total OPEC	27.3	27.9-29.9	29.0-31.6
CPE* Exports	1.7	0.5-1.5	0.0-1.0
Total	56.2	55.3-57.7	54.4-57.4

*CPE=Centrally planned economies

Source: *International Energy Annual* (Washington, D.C.: U.S. Department of Energy, September 1981).

The Turbulent 1970s

In 1970, Libyan leader Colonel Muammar Qaddafi cut back his country's production of oil. As a result of the worldwide decrease in supply and a continuing increase in demand, oil companies operating in Libya agreed to a price increase of thirty cents per barrel and a fifty-nine percent hike in local taxes. These actions triggered demands for new agreements on the part of the other oil-producing countries.[14]

Between World War II and 1970 the oil companies had experienced a steady erosion of the concessionary terms they had obtained earlier, but they still largely controlled the production and marketing of petroleum products. The situation changed when the producing countries began developing their own national oil industries, some of which then started operating in the oil exporting countries. The main weapon of the producing countries became the combination of their sovereignty and near-monopolistic ownership of the raw product. They soon had the power to act in any way they wished to control the production, distribution, and pricing of oil.

Beginning in 1970, production could no longer keep up with demand; as a direct result, oil reserves in the United States dropped sharply over a three-year period. Although the need for oil continued to grow both in the U.S. and elsewhere, no important new finds were made and, for the first time since World War II, a shortage developed. OPEC was quick to take advantage of the situation. In December 1970, the cartel demanded an increase in both the tax rate and in the base price of oil. Alarmed by the decline in domestic oil production, the U.S. Department of State invited representatives from the major oil-importing countries to Paris to convince them that it was in their best interests to agree to the increase.[15] Three months later at similar meetings in Iran, the oil-importing nations accepted the new arrangement. Major features of the Tehran Agreement, as described by an Iranian authority on oil, were:

> First, the acceptance by the oil majors, in February 1971, of a petroleum price policy based upon "collective bargaining," instead of the previous practice of unilateral determination. Second, the introduction of an "escalator clause," or parity adjustment, in income calculations—similar to the ones for wages based on general price level increases in industrial countries. Third, the establishment in December 1971 of a "real" price for oil based on putting oil on more or less the same parity with gold. And, fourth, the acceptance in March 1972 by the oil majors of the principle of local equity participation in oil-company assets and profits.[16]

In the Tehran Agreement of February 1971 and the Tripoli Agreement of April 1971, OPEC fixed oil prices at the production stage, and provided for a two and one-half percent annual increase in prices, plus an additional five cents per barrel to offset inflation.[17]

These agreements were welcomed by the U.S. Department of State, which said that "the international oil business was entering an era of good feeling, one of stability that would last at least five years."[18]

The United States demonstrated its vulnerability as the world's largest consumer of oil when it welcomed OPEC's decision to increase prices. This opened the door to later, larger price hikes. Iran, its credibility already established as a strong pro-Western nation and as an uninterrupted supplier of oil to the Western nations as well as Israel, could seize the initiative in the Tehran and Tripoli agreements without losing face. "It was Iran that took the lead in asking for higher tax rates immediately after the early Libyan agreements, and Iran was the first to get a price increase for heavy crude oils."[19]

After slow growth in 1971, petroleum production received a new impetus in 1972 when production in all countries reached approximately fifty-two million barrels per day, or about five percent more than during 1971. The increase was concentrated, however, in a relatively small number of countries, foremost among them Saudi Arabia and Iran.[20]

On the one hand, Iran increased its production to take advantage of the higher price by selling more; on the other, it took the lead again at the Geneva Conference in January 1972, raising the price of oil by twenty cents per barrel to offset the August 1971 devaluation of the U.S. dollar. To offset a second dollar devaluation in February 1973, OPEC raised the base price another fifteen cents per barrel in June 1973.[21] In August of the same year, Iran eliminated the nineteen-year-old consortium agreement covering onshore oil production. In September 1973, OPEC introduced a major increase in posted prices, and then in royalties, effective on October 16. The OPEC nations also "called for a renegotiation of the Tehran Agreement, noting that the current rate of inflation far exceeded the two and one-half percent rate contemplated in that agreement."[22] Both OPEC and the oil companies agreed to negotiate, but the discussions were never completed. In October, OPEC members in the Persian Gulf, led by Iran, unilaterally increased the price of oil from $3.01 per barrel to $5.12. "For the first time, oil exporting nations took the pricing function completely into their hands."[23] Thus, the established process of negotiations between the cartel and the industry ended as abruptly as it had begun, with an overtly political act by OPEC to end the entire process unilaterally, in violation of the agreement reached in Tehran in 1971.

A Fundamental Change

Fundamental changes in the structure of the oil industry took place following the OPEC decision to abrogate the Tehran Agreement. Henceforth, the producing countries could dictate all terms and conditions of oil sales. In this movement Iran was in the forefront—at the expense of the Arab nations. That the Iranian chairman of the Gulf "chapter" of OPEC was present at OAPEC's historic meeting in Kuwait on October 17, 1973,[24] following the end of the Yom Kippur War, was significant in itself. To many observers, the fact that Iran, a non-Arab nation, attended a meeting of an exclusively Arab cartel suggested ulterior motives on Iran's part. Subsequent events would prove these suspicions to be well-founded.

At the beginning of the Kuwait meeting, Saudi Arabia successfully resisted attempts to establish an embargo against the West. Taking the lead, Kuwait announced that it would contribute $350 million to the warring Arab states' efforts, but that it would not reduce its oil output.[25] Iran's motive in attending the OAPEC meeting seems to have influenced the Arab nations to cut off oil supplies to the pro-Israel countries supplying that nation with arms and other support. Iran's role was further demonstrated by the fact that the decision to impose an embargo was announced by the Iranian chairman of Gulf OPEC, even before the hand-written Arabic text of the resolution adopted by the Arab oil ministers was distributed to the media.[26]

While maintaining its posture of friendship toward the Western nations (at the expense of the Arab nations), Iran sought to increase its oil production and to sell it at exorbitant prices to the oil-hungry industrialized world—or even to Israel. Taking advantage of the embargo, Iran proposed to increase the posted price of oil to twenty-three dollars a barrel at a December 1973 OPEC meeting in Tehran.[27] At the direction of King Faisal, Saudi Arabian Oil Minister Sheikh Yamani not only resisted the move, but clashed directly with the Shah of Iran, who finally had to settle for $11.65 a barrel, effective January 1, 1974.[28] Although this was the officially established price, as it happens in such crisis situations, Iran sold its oil at auction for more than sixteen dollars a barrel while the embargo was in effect.[29]

The energy shortage became a problem of major proportions in many parts of the world during 1973-74. Especially hard hit were the Western industrialized nations and the Orient. The shortfall in fuel supply was partially due to the continuing rapid growth in demand for energy, particularly petroleum products. Oil consumption in Western Europe, for example, rose seven-fold from 1956 to 1973, when the Arab countries of the Middle East and North Africa reduced production in retaliation for Western support of Israel during the Yom Kippur War. The Arab nations showed their solidarity against Israel's allies by waging an "oil war" on the West and Japan. The seriousness of the energy supply shortage was underscored by the fact that in 1973 Western Europe depended on the Middle East for more than seventy percent of its oil, and Japan for some eighty percent. The United States was less dependent on imported oil, but the Arab oil embargo nevertheless had a considerable impact upon America's energy situation.

Critics in the United States charged that the energy crisis had been deliberately contrived by the large oil companies in collusion with the Arabs to generate greater profits for all. Although the companies denied this, it appears that the energy crisis was partially a reflection of political and economic pressures exerted on the oil industry as early as the 1950s. After the Suez crisis in 1956, the Iranian parliament passed the Petroleum Act of 1957, which, for the first time, recognized and encouraged the concept of joint ventures between foreign producers and host countries in the Middle East.[30]

When other nations followed Iran's lead, the oil companies realized that they would not only be paying more money for crude, but would gradually find themselves ceding control of oil operations to the producing countries. To counter-act this, the oil companies began to diversify their holdings in other parts of the world, including Southeast Asia and Australia. They also began explorations in Alaska and Canada, and increased their drilling on the outer continental shelf.

As the Middle Eastern and Caribbean countries became increasingly mili-tant, adopting strongly nationalistic policies resulting in the nationalization of their oil fields, they began to increase the price of their product. The oil companies, whether in protective reaction or through a natural rapacity for acquisition, then be-gan shifting their buying strategies, acquiring and controlling the development of competing energy sources such as coal, uranium, nuclear energy, and natural gas. The major American firms also purchased oil shales and tar sands, as well as water rights in many parts of the United States.

If the controversy over the development of the competing sources of energy was at the heart of the energy crisis, for most people the crisis was translated into immediately higher prices and widespread shortages of gasoline and fuel oil in the autumn and winter of 1973-74.

Export prices of oil roughly quadrupled in just three months. Table 4 shows this most strikingly.

TABLE 4
Price of Crude Oil, October 1973-January 1974
(in dollars)

Price Component	10-1-73	10-16-73	1-1-74
Posted Price	3.01	5.12	11.65
Royalty	0.38	0.64	1.46
Production Cost	0.12	0.12	0.12
Income	1.38	2.40	5.54
Government Revenue	1.76	3.04	7.00

Source: *Science* 184 (April 19, 1974).

Rents collected by the OPEC countries in 1973 amounted to some twenty-five billion dollars per year, growing at a rate of eleven percent or more annually[31]:

> Even before the dramatic increase in oil prices in October 1973, the Middle Eastern oil industry played a very important, but quite discreet, role in international money flow. By the mid-1960's, the presence of United States-owned oil companies in the Middle East and the marked preference of most oil-exporting countries for American-produced goods and services combined to generate large net flows of dollars into the United States.[32]

Oil Prices and the Oil-Importing Countries

High oil prices have thus far had a relatively minor impact upon the industrialized countries, since they can borrow to finance their oil imports until broader adjustments ensue. The Third World nations have no such option, but their economic hardship is not considered fundamental to the global economic order. As economist Morris A. Adelman has pointed out, "It's the underdeveloped countries that certainly are hurt as much or more than anyone by high oil prices, but they don't say a word."[33] Sooner or later the people of these countries will likely seek redress for their grievances, if their hopeless situation continues unabated. Realizing this, the oil exporters have begun to soften their attitude toward these states, providing them with economic assistance, in some cases in greater amounts on a per capita basis than the Western nations have done individually in the past.

Perhaps the hardest hit of the developed nations was Great Britain. There, bans on overtime work by coal miners, electric power workers, and railway engineers combined with the oil cutback to create a national emergency. Other Western European nations and Japan were also compelled to enact fuel-saving measures, and conservation measures were imposed on many sectors of the American economy.

The escalation in oil prices had a dramatic effect on the international trade balance and patterns of monetary debt, producing large trade deficits in almost all of the oil-importing countries. While the richer nations, those with some economic flexibility, were able to adjust to the shock of price increases, the Third World countries found themselves plunged into virtually unredeemable debt. By one account, the total worldwide debt caused by the increases was a staggering fifty-five billion dollars in 1975. Of this, the poorer states owed as much as forty percent.[34] To cope with this situation, the International Monetary Fund (IMF) established a special oil-lending or recycling facility with funds provided by the OPEC nations. Initially, OPEC contributed $9.6 billion for this purpose, lending nearly all of this to the poor countries. The developed countries created with IMF a twenty-five-billion dollar "safety net" fund for the twenty-four nations belonging to the Organization for Economic Cooperation and Development.

Whereas 1973 and 1974 were years of hostility for international oil affairs, 1975 and 1976 were years of dialogue. After a freeze on oil prices was announced by OPEC in December 1974, a further increase of ten percent was promulgated in September 1975. Saudi Arabia managed to impose a price freeze for most of 1976, but OPEC members split in December, with Saudi Arabia and the United Arab Emirates raising their oil price by five percent, and the remaining members by ten percent. The price hike announced on June 28, 1977 ranged from sixteen to twenty-four percent. Again in December 1978, an additional price increase of fourteen and one-half percent was implemented.[35]

After the most fractious meeting in OPEC's history occurred in December 1979, the cartel failed to agree upon any uniform price. As a result, no official price level was established, although, unofficially, OPEC members charged as much as sixty dollars a barrel for the same crude priced at three dollars a barrel before the Arab oil embargo of 1973. This twenty-fold price inflation of petroleum in just six years resulted in untold suffering for millions of people throughout the world.

The OPEC nations recycled their foreign exchange surpluses in three ways: (1) by buying Western consumer goods, military hardware, industrial equipment, food, and other commodities; (2) by investing their funds in development projects at home and abroad, especially in the United States and Western Europe; and (3) by lending money through official and private channels to oil-deficient poor nations.

The Uncertain 1980s

The most obvious and immediate effect of the oil price hikes of the 1970s was the massive redistribution of world wealth. While many nations sank into recession, the OPEC countries were glutted with American dollars, accumulating by the end of 1980 some $300 billion in foreign assets. At the same time, the trade surplus of OPEC countries had reached $152.5 billion, a figure that had grown to about $450 billion by 1985.[36]

By 1981-82, the oil shortage had become an oil glut, an oversupply which resulted from several important changes in the balance between supply and demand. The OPEC nations had been producing twenty-four million barrels of oil a day, while world demand had declined to less than nineteen million barrels a day. Petroleum inventories in the industrialized world rose from 4.3 billion barrels in 1979 to five billion barrels in 1981, as a direct result of the drop in consumption, by seven percent between 1979 and 1980, and by about three percent in 1981.[37]

Oil producers began restructuring their internal organizations in response to market conditions, even before the January-March (1986) crash dropped prices to ten dollars per barrel; by reducing their shut-in production capacity, they could meet the expected slow growth in demand, and force non-OPEC states into downstream markets in order to secure long-term reliable outlets for oil products.

The structure of the market will continue to evolve, but is not expected to undergo any radical changes in the 1990s. OPEC will probably regain some influence once the current supply-and-demand imbalance is settled, although its power is unlikely to rival that of the 1970s. Term contracts could also continue to play a role in balancing the expectations of buyers and sellers. Despite pressure on major oil companies to divest, they are likely to remain highly integrated—although they may become less geographically dispersed. OPEC could increase the future extent of its production.

In view of all these uncertainties, it is important that we seek to understand not only the underlying supply and demand forces that prevail in the oil market, but also the sensitivity of the oil market to changes in basic assumptions. By applying such a sensitivity analysis, a range of oil price projections can be estimated which attempts to identify a reasonable range of oil prices over the next ten years.

Even this portrayal of prices does not capture extreme market scenarios such as a supply disruption, or an oil price war, which could easily cause prices to fall outside of the projected range for at least short periods of time. Such supply disruption could force prices to rise to an unexpected high; alternatively, an oil price war could also cause prices to collapse. However, such extreme outcomes would probably be short-lived.

Nations began to look to non-OPEC sources for relief from higher prices and for a guaranteed supply—to Mexico, Great Britain, Canada, Norway, Angola, China, the Soviet Union, and Malaysia, among others. For example, in August 1981 the U.S. government, for the first time in history, signed a direct purchasing agreement with Mexico for that country to provide nearly 110 million barrels of oil to America's strategic reserve.[38] Japan began increasing its purchases from non-OPEC nations such as China, which was developing new oil fields, and Europe looked toward the Soviet Union to supply some of its additional oil.

Despite commercial incentives for the oil companies to reduce their inventory levels, a cushion of about 100 million surplus barrels remained steady throughout the 1980s. In addition, supplies from non-OPEC nations climbed above OPEC's for the first time in recent history. [See Table 5]

TABLE 5
Estimate of Oil Supply, Demand and Inventory for 1980, 1981, 1982
(Demand/Supply in million b/d, Inventory in million barrels)

Year	Demand Total	Supply Total	OPEC	Inventory Change: Non-OPEC	
1982	46.8	46.8	23.2	23.6	0
1981	47.0	46.2	23.2	23.0	-300
1980	49.4	49.9	27.6	22.3	+180

Year-to-Year Change

1982 vs. 1981	-0.2	+0.6	0	+0.6	—
1981 vs. 1980	-2.4	-3.7	-4.4	+0.7	—

Source: *Petroleum Intelligence Weekly* (January 4, 1982).

A further encouraging development is the disintegration of OPEC itself after a decade of unchallenged supremacy over oil price-setting. A major political battle raged within OPEC over how to deal with the alarming drop in prices and worldwide demand. Internal dissension, differing philosophies, and the psychological insularity of the OPEC nations resulted in a falling-out between member states.

To sustain higher prices, OPEC must trim production, and this is precisely what Saudi Arabia has tried to do. But not all members can follow suit. Indeed, some, such as Algeria, Iraq, Iran, and Indonesia, must increase production, both to maintain development plans and their debt payments to foreign lenders. Even the Saudis have so many financial commitments to Muslim nations from the income generated by its one "crop" economy that it cannot reduce production to much less than four million barrels a day. Reducing production to this level would create internal and external political and economic troubles that the Saudi rulers are anxious to avoid. They do not want to see Saudi Arabia become the next Iran.

By the mid-1980s, OPEC's worst fears had materialized—a collapse in the oil price structure and a public squabble among its members over production and pricing questions.

Before the Arab oil embargo, the Middle East determined the world's oil prices as well as the prices of other energy sources. In the future, other factors will play a much greater role, including U.S. demand, conservation efforts, and the availability of alternative energy sources at a reasonable cost.

Since roughly one-third of the world's total energy requirements are consumed by the United States, the oil-producing nations were encouraged in the 1970s to increase the price of petroleum at a staggering rate, knowing that the U.S. could afford to pay. By extracting American dollars in this way, the oil-producing nations were, so to speak, challenging the security and affluence of the United States.

The Middle East remains in turmoil. The security of oil supplies has been foremost in American foreign policy planning since the Arab oil embargo. This has become even more critical during the periods following the 1979 Iranian Revolution and the 1990 invasion of Kuwait. Instability in Iran and its war with Iraq created constant production interruptions, even though Saudi Arabia increased its output to make up for the shortfall.

Faced with a decrease in demand, OPEC members have found it increasingly difficult to agree upon even the simplest production or pricing policies. OPEC's evident disarray is due, at least partially, to differences in each country's economic and political agenda. Those with the greatest economic difficulties are the least inclined to adhere to strict production quotas.

The price of oil no longer depends on the normal workings of the economic law of supply and demand. Oil has become more of an ecostrategic commodity than simply another commercial product. The petroleum trade is more politically oriented than nearly any other business enterprise in the world—and oil resources are located mostly in pre-industrial societies which take psychic and political satisfaction in seeing the industrial giants bow and scrape. Added to these considerations is the pattern of oil production and disposition [See Table 6].

In many cases, oil production is almost entirely controlled by the host governments. The multinational oil companies have little or no financial incentive to diversify their sources; rather, they concentrate on finding relatively cheap sources of oil in a very few parts of the world. Consequently, a near monopoly in oil production has developed in the Mideast.

Because oil is one of the cheapest and most convenient sources of energy, the industrialized world changed its lifestyle by moving from a coal-based economy to one dependent on a depletable and nonrenewable source of energy. "At a time when oil was becoming more important to the countries that consume it,"[39] the producers were "seeking to industrialize their nations and build diversified economic infrastructures with oil revenues...."[40] For example, Saudi Arabia, with the largest reserves of oil, was "tying oil supplies to joint-venture projects on their soil in an attempt to attract the kinds of energy-intensive industries that make use of their only resource."[41]

TABLE 6

Crude Oil Reserves and Resources in the Market Economies
(Billions of barrels)

Country	Crude Oil Reserves OGJ	Crude Oil Reserves WO	Undiscovered Recoverable Resources FESAP	Undiscovered Recoverable Resources Mean	Undiscovered Recoverable Resources Range
Americas	117.7	119.2	NA	234.0	126-391
Canada	7.1	6.5	NA	31.4	19-48
Ecuador	1.4	0.8	1.2	1.5	1-6
Mexico	48.6	49.3	27.2	78.2	26-170
United States	83.0	83.0	NA	194.1	104-322
Venezuela	25.8	28.0	18.5	22.7	12-38
Europe	24.4	18.7	NA	23.4	13-49
United Kingdom	13.6	5.8	12.6	2.3	1-4
Other North Sea	9.0	11.5	7.0	17.9	9-34
Other Europe	1.8	1.4	NA	3.2	1-10
Middle East	398.5	373.5	419.2	173.9	72-337
Iran	48.5	37.5	62.5	26.4	11-51
Iraq	44.5	38.5	34.5	77.4	32-150
Kuwait	92.7	82.7	95.7	3.2	1-7
Qatar	3.4	4.5	7.1	0.5	1-3
Saudi Arabia	171.7	167.1	173.2	56.0	23-109
UAE	32.5	36.3	43.0	6.9	3-13
Africa	55.6	59.1	NA	58.8	28-105
Algeria	9.0	7.1	10.4	8.2	3-17
Egypt	3.2	4.0	2.4	4.6	1-12
Gabon	0.5	0.6	NA	2.0	1-6
Libya	21.1	22.8	21.0	11.7	4-25
Nigeria	16.7	16.9	12.6	8.9	2-23
Other Africa	5.1	7.7	NA	23.4	10-45
Far East	18.7	19.9	NA	33.9	16-70
Australia/N.Z.	1.6	1.6	NA	7.0	4-11
Indonesia	8.7	9.1	9.5	10.0	5-18
Total	614.9	590.5	NA	524.0	250-950

Sources: *Oil and Gas Journal* 82 (Dec. 31, 1984); *World Oil* 201 (Aug. 15, 1985); U.S. Energy Information Administration, *Foreign Energy Supply Assessment Program Series Regional Reports.*

The immediate effect of the change in the market structure was that, even with the 1986 "collapse" in crude prices, the *overall* price remained much higher then than it would have been under the "normal" market conditions which prevailed before the Arab embargo. That is, there is now very little basis upon which to predict the future price of petroleum, other than changing political scenarios which depend heavily on the fact that there is little possibility of removing politics from the oil trade. All that one can say, with any certainty, is that market conditions will remain unstable, and that the temptation for OPEC to increase its prices, either through production cuts, negotiations, or unilateral action, will be great. The question is to what extent OPEC is now the master of its own fate. In the past, when "Iran and Saudi Arabia were submissive clients of the United States,"[42] and the Western powers were able to balance the energy equation through the sanction of force, if need be, the buyers enjoyed the use of a seemingly limitless supply of cheap energy. This is no longer the case. "The energy crisis will stay with us after the political settlement of the Arab-Israeli dispute, which has been the immediate cause of the present situation."[43]

The industrialized countries were annoyed not so much by the oil price increases as by the accompanying use of oil as a political weapon; in 1973 such a situation led to the suspension of oil supplies to the United States and other Israeli allies. The Western European countries were especially hurt by the cut in Arab oil supplies and thereafter reached an understanding with the oil-producing nations.

The oil crises of the 1970s and early 1980s were decisive and historic points in the dialogue between the industrialized and developing countries. They had a positive effect on the relations between the divergent societies and gave the latter a new negotiating power that obliged others to revise their attitude and behavior toward the Third World.

Once the industrialized nations felt the effects of the oil crises, they recognized the threat posed to their supremacy in world economic and financial affairs. The oil-producing-exporting Third World countries, deriving strength from the changes taking place, seized the opportunity to impose meaningful negotiations on the industrialized countries and to insist upon a new international order that would give Third World nations the right to make their own decisions.

The bargaining leverage between oil exporters and importers has gradually shifted toward the consumers, as they slowly begin to satisfy part of their energy requirements through substitution and conservation. This is paricularly true of the United States. A shift away from a seller's market to a buyer's market, with consumers leading the rescue operation, was the hallmark of the 1980s' energy picture. Its long-term stability as we head into the mid-1990s remains to be seen.

II.

COUNTRY-COMPANY-CONSUMER RELATIONSHIPS

The world oil supply is a battered puppet manipulated by three opposing forces: the producing-exporting countries; the multinational oil companies; and the consuming nations. The producing countries are determined to use their resources to obtain political concessions and to develop their own economies at the expense of the industrialized world. As such, oil politics remains a problem that affects all nations.

A brief recapitulation of the relationships between these three forces may shed some further light on the politics of oil. During the first seventy years of the twentieth century, the producer-exporter governments were only marginally able to control their own oil. The large multinational companies owned, produced, shipped, and distributed petroleum as they liked.

Between the two World Wars, a serious search for oil was begun in the Middle East. Diplomatic infighting between the parent governments of the oil companies culminated in the 1928 Red Line Agreement, whereby an uneasy truce between American, Anglo-Dutch, and French interests in the territories of the Ottoman Empire was established.

In the meantime, Middle Eastern countries such as Iran were granting massive oil concessions to Western companies in times of extreme national weakness, allowing generous privileges and maintaining practically no control over operations and policies. The British government gave direct diplomatic and military support to the Anglo-Persian Oil Company, eventually becoming part owner. In many cases, such negotiations were never made public. Since Saudi Arabia is the largest oil producer among the OPEC nations, it is an example of the triangular relationship between country, company, and consumer.

The history of oil concessions in Saudi Arabia began in 1923, when King Abd al-Aziz ibn Abd al-Rahman Al-Saud (popularly called "Ibn Saud") granted a concession covering an area of more than 30,000 square miles in eastern Saudi Arabia to the Eastern and General Syndicate, a British-controlled consortium; but since the consortium lacked funds necessary to cover the costs of exploration, the concession was allowed to lapse four years later.

Ibn Saud, however, desperately needed funds to fight his civil war against the Hashemites in Mecca. His principal source of revenue at the time was tourism, which declined from 200,000 pilgrims in 1927 to 20,000 in 1933, partly as a result of the worldwide depression and the civil war.

Consequently, the Saudi government's bargaining power was considerably weakened by 1933. Despite some Saudi resistance, Standard Oil Company of California, through a subsidiary known as the California Arabian Standard Oil Company, obtained exclusive oil rights to a vast area of 360,000 square miles along the Persian Gulf. Signed in July 1933, the lease was to run for sixty years; the terms called for an immediate loan of £35,000 to the king, with annual rentals of £5,000 until oil was discovered in commercial quantities. The rest of Saudi Arabia remained unleased until 1939, when concessions added some 80,000 square miles to the original agreement, thus bringing the grand total of acreage owned by one company to 440,000 square miles. In return for this agreemant, Ibn Saud's government received an additional cash payment of £140,000 plus a rent of £25,000 per year.[1]

The success of California Arabian Standard, renamed Aramco in 1934, over its German, Italian, and Japanese competitors was touted as a major victory in America. The United States, which previously had no diplomatic relations with Saudi Arabia, soon established such relations: "President Roosevelt approved a proposal that the American Government purchase a controlling interest in the company; but the negotiations failed."[2]

Following the discovery and development of large petroleum reserves in Saudi Arabia, serious disputes arose after World War II concerning the financial terms of the agreement. As a result, Saudi Arabia was the first country in the Middle East to introduce a 50/50 profit-sharing formula. Once this principle was put into effect in 1950, Saudi revenues boomed. However, since the local Arabian tax could be credited against Aramco's domestic tax liabilities in the United States, Aramco's actual profits were reduced very little.

Several issues, including the abolition of special discounts on posted prices, were raised in the years following the application of the original agreement. Saudi participation on Aramco's board of directors and related Trans-Arabian Pipeline (known as Tapline) revenues were resolved to the mutual satisfaction of both parties. Apart from financial terms, another primary issue was the relinquishment of large areas covered by the original agreement. The original territory granted in 1933 to Aramco, together with the 1939 agreement to expand the concession, gave the company control over 496,000 square miles. By 1963, this had been reduced to 125,000 square miles.[3] The remaining area was to be reduced gradually at five-year intervals, so that Aramco would be left with about 20,000 square miles in its last year of operation. The reduction in Aramco's exclusive operating grant enabled the Saudi government to negotiate new agreements containing more favorable terms, with such companies as Getty Oil Company (American), Arabian Oil Companies (Japanese), AUXIRAP (French), and ENI (Italian).

As stated previously, relations between Aramco and the Saudi government have become increasingly troublesome over the years, resulting in a company that is more and more Arabian and less and less American, a process that began long before the 1973 Arab oil embargo.[4] As noted in 1974:

> By the strict letter of its contract with the Saudi government, Aramco owns concessionary rights to oil in the ground that is

worth perhaps a trillion dollars at today's prices...yet, submitting to Saudi pressure, the parent companies sold 25 percent of Aramco last year to the government for some $500 million....This left 22.5 percent each for Socal, Texaco, and Exxon, and 7.5 percent for Mobil. Under the last year's "participation" agreement, the Saudi share is to increase to 51 percent by 1982. But government officials have been talking of taking a bigger bite sooner, and not many oil executives would be surprised if Saudi Arabia eventually nationalized the company.[5]

Saudi Arabia's physical control of oil means, in effect, that the only right Aramco and other companies now have is to produce, buy, and sell at terms dictated by the host government. However, relatively speaking, relations between Saudi Arabia and the oil companies have been less acrimonious than relations of either group with Iran or Iraq. Still, Saudi Arabia has brought strong pressure upon Aramco in order to modify the terms of the original concession.

The Saudis have complained publically about their lack of effective control over Aramco. However, following the application of the 50/50 principle, oil revenues to Saudi Arabia doubled within a year, rising from $56.7 million in 1950 to $110 million in 1951. Since then, oil revenues have escalated steadily, reaching a total of $2.734 billion in 1972. This is due to higher oil exports and higher crude oil revenues used in calculating the Saudi income tax. The 1973-74 oil crisis increased Saudi petroleum revenues to $22.6 billion in 1974, and to $104.2 billion in 1980[6], a staggering surge in just ten years.

During the postwar period, foreign investment in oil production has been greatest in the Kingdom of Saudi Arabia, and the resulting investment growth rapid. The operating company of Aramco started its activities in Saudi Arabia in 1933 with an original operating capital of $500,000, which increased to $700,000 in 1936. By 1946, Aramco had invested some $115 million in Saudi oil, and by 1956 the total value of Aramco's gross fixed assets was some $608.7 million. After the deduction of $269.4 million for depreciation and amortization, Aramco's net assets were $339.3 million by the end of 1956, which, after the addition of the company's net working capital of $67.7 million, plus miscellaneous assets of $64.3 million, totalled $471.3 million.[7] From 1933 to 1973, Aramco's total investment in Saudi Arabia exceeded two billion dollars.[8]

There are widely differing (and disputed) estimates available on investment in oil exploration and production. But estimates on a country-by-country basis are not readily ascertainable except for figures cited in a wide variety of publications. This is because the oil companies provide such figures only on a regional basis, restricting, as trade secrets, specific figures on investments in individual countries. However, the U.S. Department of State does compile some investment figures on a country-by-country basis. The figure of two billion dollars cited above from a Department of State publication as the total of Aramco's investments in Saudi Arabia is a reasonable amount, since the company later sold its Saudi interests for exactly that price. Investments by other foreign companies in Saudi Arabia are of more recent origin, and are considered negligible compared to Aramco's forty years of extensive operations there.

By using existing technology, an established petroleum reservoir has a certain volume of recoverable oil; any improvement in this technology increases the amount of recoverable oil at a specified cost. Volume and cost increases are, by and large, measurable and subject to rational calculation. The possible percentage spread between natural and stimulated oil recovery provides an incentive to perfect and to use improved machinery. This technology has had a dramatic impact on Saudi Arabian oil poduction.

The production of oil can logically be linked with exploration. In economic terms, the business of oil exploration, development, production, and transportation is fairly capital-intensive. With sufficient volume, pipelines are more efficient than other means of land transportation. Tankers and pipelines are also used to move both petroleum products and unprocessed crude, although the latter accounts for some three-quarters of the oil transported in international trade.[9]

Aramco's Experience

Since our principal interest lies with Saudi Arabia's political policies, rather than with the economic and technical spheres of Saudi oil production and transportation, we will limit our discussion of oil operations to a brief account of Aramco's experiences while operating in Saudi Arabia under a supplemental, sixty-year concessionary agreement, concluded in 1939, six years after the original agreement. Aramco is owned by four American corporations[10] in the following proportions: Standard Oil Company of California—thirty percent; Texas Company—thirty percent; Standard Oil Company (New Jersey)—thirty percent; and Socony Mobil Oil Company—ten percent.

From the viewpoint of the United States and other industrialized nations, Saudi Arabia is a primary energy source, since it contains the largest proven oil reserves in the world.[11] Saudi Arabia is the leading oil producer in the Middle East and the third largest in the world after the United States and the Soviet Union, with some 315 billion barrels of oil in reserves.[12]

After the initial discovery of oil, several years are required to prepare it for production. From a relatively modest beginning in 1933, Aramco's Saudi Arabian oil venture has developed into one of the largest in the world. The first commercial oil field was discovered at Dammam in 1938; by the end of 1951, it was producing 90,000 barrels a day. In 1940, the Abu Hadriya and Abqaiq fields were first explored, and by the end of 1951 they were producing 590,000 barrels a day. Qatif and Ain Dar were developed in 1945, with a daily production of 20,000 and 150,000 barrels, respectively. Other oil fields were discovered in 1949 and 1951. By 1955, 154 wells in Saudi Arabia were averaging 965,000 barrels of oil production per day.[13] Saudi production reached 8.29 million barrels of oil per day before the 1973 Arab-Israeli War,[14] and could boost its official reserves by twenty percent following the 1990 discovery of extensive new reserves.

Aramco built some 330 miles of pipeline, ranging from ten-to-thirty inches in diameter and from eighteen-to-forty-five miles in length. In addition to its main Trans-Arabian Pipeline—the famous Tapline, 1,070 miles in length—there are additional pipelines that bring crude from the fields to the Bahrain refineries and to tanker loading stations along the Persian Gulf. By the end of 1945, the refinery at Ras Tanura had been expanded to a 50,000-barrel-per day capacity, and, after further expansion, 1954's deliveries amounted to 79.8 million barrels. In general, Saudi Arabian oil exports are moved by pipelines to sea terminals, and then transported by supertankers to the world market.

The legal owner of Saudi Arabian oil is the royal family, represented by the king as a kind of "Chairman of the Board." The absence of general mining or petroleum laws in Saudi Arabia necessitated negotiations with the American companies over the formulation of specific terms of the concessions.

The concessionary arrangements provided extensive rights and privileges to the oil companies and guaranteed for them the continuation of their operations. Before the changes that took place in 1950, a United Nations report noted:

> The terms of their concessions...give the foreign companies a freedom of action which substantially insulates them from the economy of the Middle Eastern countries. Output is determined by considerations of world, rather than local, conditions....The foreign exchange derived from sales of oil accrues to the petroleum companies and is, in large measure, retained by them. Hence the impact of oil operations on Middle Eastern producing countries is mainly indirect....[15]

On December 30, 1950, Saudi Arabia and Aramco instituted a major change in the concession under which Aramco was operating by concluding a profit-sharing agreement, commonly known as the 50/50 agreement. "The agreement was of great importance in as much as it set a precedent for similar formulas in other oil-producing countries of the Middle East."[16]

By the royal decree of February 21, 1973, the participation agreement signed on December 20, 1972 was ratified, providing Saudi Arabia with an initial participation of twenty-five percent in oil production, pipeline, storage, delivery, and export facilities. In addition, beginning in January 1978, the Saudis were entitled to an annual increment of five percent with a final increment of six percent, which culminated in a participation level of fifty-one percent by 1982.[17] The agreement also gave the Saudis the right to play an active role in the management of Aramco, requiring the company to move the seat of its board of directors from New York to Dharan. Saudi Arabia, however, made little overall use of the joint venture provision, although at one point it did seem to be heading in that direction.

Although the basic framework of the new agreement remained unchanged, there were a number of important alterations in the terms of the original agreement that favor Saudi Arabia, such as the one outlined above; the Saudis desired such changes in order to obtain larger profits from their own natural resources.

The apparent reluctance of the oil companies to cooperate with Saudi Arabia in the past has created an atmosphere of mutual suspicion. The situation began to change as Saudi Arabia slowly started to diversify its oil concessions, awarding contracts to French, Japanese, British, and Italian companies. At the same time, Saudi Arabia began to develop its own national oil company.[18]

Sensing this change, Aramco adopted a policy of becoming increasingly more "Arabian," and helped the Saudis to implement their embargo against their own government. Aramco even backed the producers' policy of massive price hikes.[19]

Until 1950, the oil companies dictated the terms of the agreements to the host governments. In other words, the consuming nations set the energy policies of the oil-producing countries. Now that the producers are united under the banner of regional oil organizations, they are determined to maintain control of their own economies and cooperate with outsiders only on their own terms.

The New Triangle

Basically, this change in company-host-consumer relationships begets a new triangle: the producing-exporting countries on the first side, the national and transnational oil companies on the second side, and the consuming nations on the third side.

During the early 1970s, the demand for oil increased in the major consuming countries, as the table following indicates:

TABLE 7
Oil Imports to Consuming Countries, 1970-73
(thousand barrels daily)

Country	1971	1972	1973	% Increase 1968-73
United States	3,930	4,740	6,205	17.2
Western Europe	13,520	14,065	15,310	7.9
Japan	4,720	4,815	5,760	13.5

Source: British Petroleum Co., *Statistical Review of the World Oil Industry*, London, 1973.

The oil companies met this increased demand from their existing sources of supply. They were reluctant to invest in new exploration ventures, since the producing countries were opting for participation in such ventures, or even outright nationalization of such resources. Originally, Saudi Arabia devised a twenty-five percent participation arrangement, which was soon adopted by the other Gulf states. The share of participation was increased from twenty-five to sixty percent until, finally, during the 1970s, the remaining forty percent of Aramco's ownership was absorbed entirely by the Saudis.[20] The full participation agreement was, in effect, an attempt to make Aramco a mere production contractor for Saudi Arabia. Apart from its immediate effects, this trend represented a broad movement among the oil-producing Third World countries to negotiate full participation agreements and/or eventual nationalization.

Taking further advantage of the changed political realities in the world, the oil-producing countries, with an overwhelming majority of United Nations members (the vote tally was 120 in favor, six against, including the United States), adopted a Charter of Economic Rights and Duties of States and proclaimed, on December 13, 1974, the right of countries to control their natural resources and to take over foreign firms.[21] The vote symbolized an end to American control of the United Nations, and simultaneously of the world oil industry. On the same day, OPEC, meeting in Vienna, decided to replace its multiple-price system with a flat-price structure. A key element in this new system was the elimination of posted prices, which were only a reference point in the computation of the producers' taxes and royalties. At the same time, the price of oil was increased by thirty cents per barrel, thereby boosting the producing governments' revenues from $9.74 a barrel to $10.12.[22]

The real effect of the new system was the shifting of profit margins from the multinational oil companies to the host countries. In the past, the companies have compensated for such profit cuts by raising their product prices to the consumer. Under such circumstances, higher oil prices are in the companies' best interests, as two oil analysts, Elizabeth Monroe and Robert Mabro, have pointed out:

> In theory a high price suits a commercial firm engaged in expensive operations all over the world provided that its profit margin remains; but in fact the companies' net incomes rose enormously thanks to the 1974 prices, they were worried about the reduced demand these prices presaged, and about the changing shape of their industry.[23]

In any event, the oil companies had no alternative but to concur with the 1973-74 price hikes and to maintain a low profile in the host countries. These were days of great uncertainty for the oil companies and, in their attempt to survive, they diversified their operations into substitute energy resources and other non-related fields. For example, Shell and Exxon entered into both the nuclear and the coal businesses, Mobil purchased the retail establishment Montgomery Ward,[24] and the Atlantic Richfield Company (ARCO) conducted a huge research project on the need for public transportation, with the hope of developing business there. Oil companies are even diversifying their operations abroad: Aramco has undertaken an electrification program for the whole of eastern Saudi Arabia, and is also designing, building, and operating a four and one-half billion dollar gas and gas-liquid system to serve several planned industrial centers in Saudi Arabia.[25]

How can the nations of the world cope with this new situation? The oil-producers' income is anyone's guess. but the massive price increases of the 1970s certainly have transferred billions of dollars from the industrialized countries to the Middle East. "At minimum, OPEC as a whole, after satisfying its import needs, disposed of a surplus of...$650 billion by 1980 and a projected $1,200 billion by 1985."[26] Since the oil price collapse of the mid-1980s, OPEC no longer has a huge surplus of funds.

The Most Severely Affected Countries

The high cost of oil in the 1970s affected non-producing Third-World states, the so-called Most Severely Affected (MSA) countries, to a much greater degree than the industrialized West. Although their per capita consumption of oil is small, their huge populations have meant that, in order to satisfy their energy needs, they have had to deplete their meager financial resources at rates which are ruinous to the possibility of financial development and independence. Bangladesh is one notable example: lacking oil or any other vital resources of its own, Bangladesh depends very heavily on the Arab nations' handouts for its mere survival. It has been reduced to this status because it has no choice. The oil-producing nations have recognized the problem by giving them some financial assistance, or by providing petroleum at reduced prices. This largesse has not been sufficient, however, to stop the general economic deterioration of these countries as they have struggled to pay their energy bills.

At the other extreme is the United States, almost a world unto itself. It could also possibly remain a host unto itself, as it once was, requiring little outside energy assistance, but due to unwise consumption policies, waste, failure to develop substitute energy sources, and inertia, it remains heavily dependent on foreign oil supplies. Bangladesh, one of the poorest of the poor, has become insolvent as a result of paying its petrobills: the United States, financially one of the strongest nations, has been seriously weakened for many of the same reasons.

In short, the attempt by the oil-producing nations to transfer wealth from the industrialized world to the Middle East and elsewhere, while apparently successful in the short term, has also simultaneously damaged the economies of other Third World states, and threatens to injure the world's basic financial structures. The oil companies, principal actors in the past, are merely silent spectators now. The further attempt by OPEC to link the price of oil to the prices of other major goods, including food and manufacturing, will inevitably make the poor nations even poorer. Although the alleged intention of the oil producers is to protect their oil revenues against currency inflation in the industrial countries, their attempt to index oil prices with other essential commodities without regard for the cost of production and market conditions has struck a severe blow to prospects for the Third World's economic survival. Like dying patients in a hospital, unable to help themselves, the poorer countries remain comatose and paralyzed, hopeful that the oil-producing nations will somehow come to their relief in this, the "eleventh hour." Meanwhile, the relationship between producing and consuming governments has become bitter. As a result, the world is facing a calamity, either now or in the near future (i.e., the next twenty years), unless the industrialized nations reexamine their profligate energy policies, and begin developing substitute sources of energy.

Nationalization and Expropriation

One of the approaches taken by the oil-producing countries to "correct" the early concession agreements was expropriating the property of multinational oil companies. Nationalization of foreign assets came to embody these countries' nationalistic sentiments concerning the utilization of their own wealth:

> Nationalization, expropriation, or requisitioning shall be based on grounds or reasons of public utility, security, or the national interest....In accordance with the rules in force in the state, taking such measures in the exercise of its sovereignty and in accordance with international law.[27]

Many countries found no other way to rectify the early oil agreements except by resorting to drastic measures. But Saudi Arabia, the most moderate and pragmatic of these states, took control of its resources through mutual consultations and agreements with Aramco, and by paying financial compensation to that company.

The terms of new concessions are now a matter of public record, and there is a relatively clear picture of the oligopolistic organization of the international oil industry. Our debate is less with the facts than with the fairness of the terms which the oil-producing countries have conceded to the oil companies. From a global point of view, there is far more at stake here than simply a shift in the balance of economic advantage between the oil companies and the producing-exporting countries.

In the 1960s, OPEC remained largely a defensive organization. This weakness allowed the major oil companies to retain their dominant position in the sale of petroleum worldwide. They were helped by the fact that many of the oil-producing countries were "client states" of the West. The increasing demand for cheap energy prompted the entry of many independent firms into the field, firms which managed successfully to compete with the majors. The industrialized countries had good reason to be complacent: oil supply was both cheap and plentiful—and it was increasingly essential to the economic well-being of the Western world.

The main force that dominated energy in the 1970s was the continuous, rapid rise in demand in both developed and developing nations, capitalist and communist nations alike. The world entered this decade almost totally unprepared for concerted action by the oil-producing countries. The Arab oil embargo of 1973-74 symbolized the way in which the power balance in the world had shifted. Not only had the producing countries learned how to improve their financial return by raising oil prices, but they also were no longer vulnerable to the kinds of pressures imposed upon them in the past. The 1970s and most of the 1980s also enabled OPEC to wring ever greater concessions from the mighty oil companies.

Given the symbiotic relationship between major oil companies and their home governments, it was once not unusual for the latter to come to the former's aid with military and financial assistance. Gunboat diplomacy effectively scared the governments and people of the oil-producing countries into cooperating with the consumer's representatives, the large oil companies. Now that those days are gone, the multinational corporations must rely far more on their commercial acumen than on the political clout and unusable military might of their parent governments.

"For...the major oil companies the good old days were those ten or twelve years which immediately followed the Second World War."[28]   Oil prices from World War II to the Suez War in 1956 were determined mostly by large companies which could not only post a price but sell at that price. At that time, nearly all OPEC oil was produced by major organizations that maintained a monopolistic control over the world's oil market. This was accomplished by their ownership of affiliated refining and marketing companies in oil-importing countries.

Following the 1956 Suez War, the last colonial ventures of the Western powers were doomed, when the U.S. failed to support the French and British expeditionary force. Thereafter, a few independent oil companies began seeking and acquiring oil concessions in the Middle East, although not at the low prices the majors had obtained in the "good old days." New patterns began emerging, "for instance, the 75/25 principle whereby foreign elements had to put up the risk capital in the exploration stage and on discovery had to give fifty percent"[29] of the oil discovered to the indigenous partners.   In the words of Morris A. Adelman, a leading petroleum expert:

> The United States government, as trustee for the customers—and home government to most of the companies—compelled them to do what would not otherwise have happened, at least not so much so soon. After 1950, when the pressure disappeared, we see an actual reversal, with prices rising by perhaps 20 percent through 1956.[30]

The seven majors, or, as their adversaries called them, "the seven sisters," were strongly supported in the political arena by the U.S. Department of State.[31] The twenty-to-thirty "newcomers" operated more or less independently, and while these independents sometimes found it difficult to market their products in the oil world controlled by the majors, they were ultimately successful in breaking the monopoly of the "seven sisters."

The development of the independents (or "minors,") was followed by the emergence of national oil companies sponsored by the producing nations. Usually, the nationals have tried to export their product in areas such as Eastern Europe where they do not compete directly with the majors. Their limited operations in the world market cannot yet be considered competitive with the majors or even the minors, but are still viewed by the producing states as symbols of each country's national aspirations to gain a place in the sun of international politics.[32]

The Arab use of petrodiplomacy changed the supply/demand ratio and created a partially artificial oil famine in the world market. Within a few months the traditional buyers' market had changed completely to a sellers' market. The multinational oil companies, fearing the total loss of their business, changed sides immediately, and alligned themselves with the oil producers. From their point of view, this was the sensible thing to do, since they lacked support from their home governments in their overseas operations, support which they had traditionally received in the past. The opportunity for the international oil companies to exercise vertical control over all aspects of oil production through the use of capital investment and technical and administrative expertise, is over. It is not likely to return.

III.

ARAB OIL AS A VOLATILE WEAPON

The oil-exporting Arab countries had litle to do with the development of their own oil industries, as most of them were developed by outside investors. Today, however, the OAPEC nations control their oil resources, and the militant attitudes of some pose a serious threat to the continuous flow of oil to other nations. Without its oil, the Middle East would collectively have little influence on international affairs; even with petroleum, these nations individually can have minimal impact on the world stage.

None of the oil-exporting countries at present has a dominant position in the international oil market, although Saudi Arabia's oil reserves make it a formidable power, providing the leverage that sometimes, but not always, allows it to sway OAPEC's policies. This influence is mitigated by the fact that not all of the OAPEC nations can afford to follow a specific supply-and-demand ratio in production over a long period of time, due to their foreign debts and larger development needs. Only Saudi Arabia, Kuwait, and Libya can increase or lower production to any significant degree, to keep supply reasonably balanced with demand. The huge accumulation of petrodollars by these three countries gives them the key to OAPEC's internal politics, and even to OPEC's ultimate success or failure in the international arena. The driving force for change in the Arab world is oil, which is not only reshaping the structure and character of its own society, but also radically changing the economic and political significance of the region to the rest of the world.

The concept of using oil as a diplomatic weapon is as old as the Arab-Israeli conflict itself. Anticipating Western support of the Israeli cause, the Arab League passed a set of resolutions in June 1946, one of which called for the denial of oil to the West.[1] When fighting broke out in Palestine in May 1948, the decision to embargo the West's supply of Arab oil was not implemented, largely due to opposition by Saudi Arabia, "which believed that a commercial oil operation should be divorced from political considerations."[2] Since all Arab oil at that time was being produced by the international oil companies, the Arab League suddenly realized that its member-states had no voice in deciding the level of production, price, and export of the commodity.

Nevertheless, this premature attempt to use oil as a diplomatic weapon in the settlement of the Arab-Israeli conflict met with some success, as George Lenczowski notes:

In a gesture of defiance toward Israel and out of solidarity with other Arab states, Iraq stopped the movement of oil by pipeline to the Israeli-held Haifa terminal and caused construction of the parallel line between Kirkuk and Haifa to cease...and... boycott measures against Israel by the Arab League gradually affected the transactions of a number of oil companies with Israel.[3]

Of the four Arab-Israeli wars so far, oil figured significantly in all but that of 1948. In 1956, when Egypt nationalized the Suez Canal, Great Britain and France declared war against Egypt. When Israel joined Britain and France, the second Arab-Israeli war started. The Arab countries not only blocked the flow of oil to Israel, but also to the Mediterranean via the Suez Canal; pipelines from Iraq and Saudi Arabia were closed; some were blown up by nationalist elements in retaliation for the tripartite attack on Egypt. The closing of the Suez Canal and the embargo on the shipment of Arab oil to Great Britain and France had serious consequences for their economies, immediately increasing prices. The oil companies now had to obtain much of their product from the United States. The little Middle Eastern oil for sale was transported via the Cape of Good Hope, again entailing additional shipping costs. As a result, oil rationing was introduced in Western Europe.

During the Suez War, in a strange pairing, the United States found itself "allied" with the Soviet Union, and ultimately played the key role in the conflict by calling upon Great Britain, France, and Israel to cease hostilities and withdraw their forces. Directly or indirectly, the two superpowers also urged Egypt and the other Arab countries to abandon their embargo on the shipment of oil to their adversaries. Consequently, Arab attempts to use oil as a diplomatic weapon ultimately failed, again without achieving the desired goal of permanently resolving the Arab-Israeli conflict. The six-month oil embargo had no lasting impact on the Western European economy.

By 1967, when the third round of the conflict began, Mideast oil had become even more important to the industrialized world, due to the fact that oil had replaced almost entirely the use of coal. As the war broke out, Egyptian President Gamal Abdel Nasser announced that Great Britain and the United States had joined Israel in the attack upon the Arabs.[4] He also said that the U.S. Sixth Fleet had helped Israel attack Egyptian airports and military bases. Although these accusations were false, the Arabs took them seriously. Notices were issued to the oil companies to cease exporting oil to the countries blacklisted by the Arabs, including Great Britain and the United States. West Germany was added to the embargo list for its sale of gas masks to Israel. For the first time, Arab oil-producing nations shut down virtually their entire oil production. In Saudi Arabia and Kuwait, "bands of saboteurs assembled with explosives, ready to destroy the big companies' installations once and for all."[5] Before the brigands could act, Arab troops occupied the oil fields. The soldiers were ordered to stop the flow of oil, but their presence actually prevented independent sabotage by radical groups. The pattern of the 1956 oil embargo was repeated when the Suez Canal closed again, in 1967.

The European economy was not as badly hurt as in 1956, because petroleum was imported from Libya, Algeria, and Venezuela to make up the difference. The United States also exported oil to Great Britain and other European countries to help them meet the crisis.

Because of several factors, the oil embargo lasted just two weeks. First, because of their own inaccurate propaganda, the Arabs decided to use their oil weapon as the only apparent alternative to inaction. Second, within a few days it was clear that none of the Arab nations had the financial strength to carry on the embargo without obtaining money from the oil companies. "Saudi Arabia was the first to feel the pinch acutely....King Faisal was informed by his finance minister that there was no more money in the till, and that for once Aramco was unable to help."[6] Finally, an Arab summit conference held in Khartoum shortly after the war decided that oil should be used "positively" as a political weapon, the implication being that their approach in 1967 had been based on false information. In any event, it is worth referring to a statement made by the undersecretary of the Kuwaiti Ministry of Foreign Affairs, who said:

> Kuwait has always subscribed to the notion that oil should be used as a weapon in the confrontation with Israel, and has, however, applied this notion ever since it established the Kuwaiti fund for Arab Economic Development, which strengthens the Arab economy by financing development projects that have helped and continue to help Arab steadfastness....It is not in anyone's interest to use oil negatively.[7]

The situation in 1967 had been badly mishandled. "Injudiciously used, the oil weapon loses much if not all of its importance and effectiveness," said Sheikh Yamani.[8] On the Arab manipulation of oil, he said further that, "If we do not use it properly, we are behaving like someone who fired a bullet into the air, missing the enemy, and allowed it to rebound on himself."[9]

The oil shots missed the targets because, primarily, the United States was not hurt by them. On the contrary, the embargo enabled the international oil companies to make handsome profits by selling American, Venezuelan, and North African oil at inflated prices. Secondly, despite the closure of the Suez Canal, the oil companies were able to supply their customers in Europe without much difficulty. Thirdly, no quota ceilings were imposed by the Arab governments, which encouraged overlifting of oil from the Mediterranean and other ports.

"Oil is a formidable weapon if it is used properly," said King Hussein, ruler of the oil-less Kingdom of Jordan.[10] The proper and positive use of oil as a weapon of diplomacy can only be made if sufficient funds are available to sustain a long and arduous embargo, and to help the have-nots in the rank-and-file of the Arab world.

Following the June War of 1967, the entire atmosphere of inter-Arab politics changed. Although the Arabs were not motivated by international considerations, they began giving serious thought to the pan-Arab mystique. The message of military defeat reached equally to the belligerent and nonbelligerent: "There could hardly be a competition for prestige when there was no prestige remaining."[11] Self-interest and rivalry were no longer strong factors in deterring concrete action aimed at unity and sharing wealth. The Arab oil countries have been making financial contributions to the oil-short Arab states continuously since the 1967 war.

The countries involved directly in the conflict with Israel were Egypt, Syria, and Jordan. These were not oil-producing states, although both Egypt and Syria had enough wells to supply part of their domestic needs. These countries called upon their larger oil-producing neighbors to use their oil as a weapon in the struggle against Israel. For example, "In 1967, Saudi Arabia cut the flow of oil involuntarily, under pressure by Nasser, and therefore did not enforce the measure strictly and cancelled it as soon as possible."[12] However, pressure or no pressure, the Arab nations in general responded to the call of Arab unity, and invoked their embargo weapon against Israel or the West whenever the occasion demanded.

As pointed out previously, the structure of the world's oil industry changed in the early 1970s because of the disappearance of surplus production in the United States, and the now-growing direct control of the multinational oil companies under OPEC. The U.S. and other industrialized non-Communist countries of the world became increasingly dependent on a free-flowing supply of oil from the Arab world. The industry in the United States continuously stressed the significance of Arab oil in maintaining American growth, singling out Saudi Arabia as the most important source of supply to the Western Hemisphere.

In 1972, the Economic Council of the Arab League launched a study of the strategic use of Arab economic power vis-à-vis Israel and the energy-consuming world. The report did not call for an embargo, noting that restrictive oil production would bring pressure on the consuming nations to alter their uncompromising support for Israel.[13] Resultingly, Saudi Arabia and other Arab nations came under pressure to reduce their oil production.

Upon the advice of King Faisal, Egyptian President Anwar Sadat expelled the Soviets from Egypt so that the United States could exert pressure on Israel to withdraw to its 1967 borders. Clearly, the Nixon administration failed to fulfill the commitments it had made to Faisal. As a final attempt at a peaceful settlement, Sadat sent his national security adviser, Hafez Ismail, to Washington to prevail upon President Nixon to make good his promises. It was at this time that Israeli Premier Golda Meir visited Washington, and President Nixon yielded to Israeli pressure by making public his intention of supplying Israel with Phantom jets—and infuriated both Sadat and Faisal.

The 1973 Oil Embargo

King Faisal, who had gained considerable prestige and respect in the Arab and Muslim world, was much embarrassed by the renewed American desire to supply sophisticated arms and equipment to Israel. Having lost face with Sadat and the other Arab leaders, in April 1973 he dispatched Sheikh Yamani to Washington, where his oil minister explicitly linked oil and politics for the first time. Yamani told American officials that it was impossible for Saudi Arabia to work against the interests of its Arab neighbors. American officials did not take Yamani seriously, ignoring him in the belief that he was speaking for himself and not for King Faisal. To remove these misgivings, Faisal told Aramco's president in Saudi Arabia that he was "not able to stand alone much longer"[14]; pressure was building to use oil as a weapon. Following King Faisal's warning, Aramco launched a campaign to influence government circles in Washington, urging that the United States follow an even-handed policy in the Middle East. Later, the Aramco officials cited the powerful Jewish lobby in the United States as an effective barrier to the company's success in changing America's policy of informal partiality toward Israel.

On May 15, 1973, the twenty-fifth anniversary of Israel's creation, Algeria, Kuwait, Iraq, and Libya stopped oil production for a short time as a symbolic message to the world that Arab oil producers could—and would—use their oil as an effective weapon against oil-consuming nations. About the same time, Libya, taking action against foreign holdings, nationalized the American company Bunker Hunt, assuming majority interests in Occidental and Oasis. However, as Saudi Arabia maintained an attitude of moderation and traditional friendship with the United States, its policy clearly was one of wait-and-see.

The oil-producing Arab nations had already increased oil revenues and oil production beyond any domestic needs in social and economic development. The Saudis now began preparing plans for a selective embargo, even before war broke out in October. On September 4, the *Christian Science Monitor* published an interview with King Faisal and his son, Prince Saud, which had originally appeared in a Lebanese newspaper. The article stated:

> Oil is not an artillery shell, but an enormous weapon. All economic weapons need study and time for effectiveness to appear. Talk of using the oil weapon...makes it sound as if we were threatening the whole world, while it is understood that our purpose is to bring pressure to bear on America...but America would be the last to get hurt, because the United States will not depend on Arab oil before the end of the 1970s, whereas Japan and Western Europe depend on it now. What benefits are there...from arousing the fears of the Europeans and Japanese at a time when they are showing greater sympathy for us?...Arab policy is called upon today to persuade the American and European citizen that his interests are with the rights of the Arabs and that we do not intend to harm him, but that it is the policy of his government that is creating the confrontation (with Israel). We must tell the American and European people that we want to defend ourselves, not harm them.[15]

When war broke out on October 6, it looked at first as though the Arabs would not need to use their oil weapon. However, as the war turned against the

Arabs, the oil ministers of OAPEC held a meeting in Kuwait on October 17 to consider using oil as an arm in their struggle to liberate the lands occupied by Israel in 1967. In their attempt to bail out Egypt and Syria, which were directly fighting Israel, the Arab oil ministers concluded:

> Considering that the ultimate goal of the current struggle is the liberation of the Arab territories occupied by Israel in the 1967 war, and the restoration of the legitimate rights of the Palestinian people in accordance with United Nations resolutions;
>
> Considering that the United States is the principal and foremost source of Israeli power that enabled it to continue occupying their territories;
>
> Considering that the industrial nations have a responsibility of implementing the United Nations resolutions;
>
> Considering that the economic situation of many Arab oil producing countries does not justify raising oil production, although they are willing to make an increase to meet the demand in those industrial nations that are committed to cooperation in the task of liberating occupied territories;
>
> That each Arab oil exporting country immediately cut its oil production by a rate not less than five percent from the September production level, and a further increase of five percent from each of the following months, until such time as the international community compels Israel to relinquish occupied Arab lands, and to levels that will not undermine their economies or their national Arab obligations.[16]

As a result, October 17 was a banner day in the history of the world's energy crisis—the oil states of Saudi Arabia, Kuwait, Iraq, Libya, Algeria, the United Arab Emirates, Qatar, Bahrain, Egypt, and Syria joined in the war against Israel by imposing an immediate cut in oil production. The next day, Saudi Arabia independently cut production by ten percent. The day after, Libya announced that it would raise the price of its oil by an additional twenty-eight percent, even though there had been several small price increases before the October War had begun. Iraq announced a seventy percent increase in the price of oil. When the oil ministers met again in Kuwait on November 4, they decided that the initial reduction in output would be twenty-five percent of the September level and that a further cut of five percent would be made during each of the following months to "levels that will not undermine their economies or their national Arab obligations."[17] Meanwhile, following massive deliveries of American arms to Israel, a total halt of oil exports to the United States and the Netherlands was announced by Saudi Arabia, the United Arab Emirates, Kuwait, and Algeria, and the actual diminution in supplies to other industrialized nations varied between five and ten percent.

While regretting the move, the Arab oil ministers said that Israel had contributed to a five percent reduction in the flow of oil to the world by bombing an oil terminal in Syria and thus forcing a fifty percent reduction of the flow of oil through the Trans-Arabian Pipeline. The ministers appealed to the world community as a whole, and to the American people in particular, to "help us in our struggle" against occupation. Although the Arab countries wished to cooperate with all, and the oil producers were ready to supply the world with its petroleum needs, the ministers said, the time had come to condemn Israel's aggression.

The Arab nations' willingness to use their oil resources as a not-so-subtle weapon of diplomacy has been attributed to their enhanced concern about Israel, and to their increased bargaining power from accumulated petrodollars:

> As long as Israel had been hemmed in within the pre-1967 boundaries, surrounded by a ring of Arab states that contained it and threatened to roll it back, countries like Saudi Arabia, Kuwait, and Iraq could feel completely safe from any Israeli threat. Whatever contribution they made to the Arab cause against Israel was made purely on the grounds of pan-Arab considerations. But as Israel overwhelmingly...demonstrated a...capacity to hurt them in a significant way....Their concern with Israel...became an investment in their own security.[18]

Following the death of Nasser and the subsequent improvement in Saudi-Egyptian relations, King Faisal demonstrated his increased ability to guide his country's foreign policy more independently:

> In the past Faisal feared that once he had sprung the "oil weapon," others, particularly Nasser, might be able to arrogate to themselves the right to decide when and how it was to be used.[19]

The Arab states administered the embargo in their own individual ways. Saudi Arabia separated the world into three categories: (1) friendly countries; (2) unfriendly countries; and (3) all others.[20] The friendly countries included Great Britain, France, Spain, Pakistan, Malaysia, and all the non-oil producing Arab nations. The unfriendly countries were to receive no oil at all, while the friendly countries were to continue receiving oil at pre-embargo levels. "When they had been served," said King Faisal, "then whatever was left might be distributed to the rest of the world."[21]

As the Arab embargo went into effect panic ensued in Europe and Japan; the situation was less severe in the United States, but serious concern was noticeable during the crisis. Both radical and conservative Arab states embargoed oil against the United States, the Netherlands, and, most ardently, Israel. Saudi Arabia, the least radical of all, wanted to put pressure on the United States to minimize its support for Israel. Iraq, one of the most radical, believed that Europe, except for those countries directly supporting Israel, and Japan, which was increasingly friendly toward the Arab cause, should be supplied with oil. The Arabs knew that nothing spectacular could be expected from the United States, which had declared a pro-Israeli position for domestic political reasons.

With Europe and Japan gravely threatened by their heavy dependence on Arab oil, they were simultaneously subjected to severe Arab diplomatic pressure—or "blackmail," as the Western news media termed it. At various times, the Arabs issued ultimatums and oral threats that a stringent oil embargo would be imposed on all of Europe and Japan if Western policies toward Israel did not change. Indeed, both Great Britain and West Germany, long known for their pro-Israeli postures, banned arms shipments to all combatants, including Israel. London even refused to allow U.S. transport planes to land on British territory, and Bonn protested the shipment of American arms from Germany to Israel. Thus, a rift developed in NATO, and the United States was left alone in its support of Israel.[22] The European governments denied that they had been threatened in any way by the Arabs. As the British foreign secretary said, "There has been a great deal of talk recently about a submission to Arab blackmail....The Arabs have made no demand on us and we have offered no price."[23] The fact is that while Great Britain and other European countries were adopting a neutral position toward the Arab-Israeli conflict, the supply of oil from the Arab world was becoming progressively more assured. As London's *Sunday Times* pointed out, "Britain's oil is safe—if we behave ourselves."[24] Another influential power in Europe, France, because of its special relationship with the Arabs, expected better treatment from them and, indeed, did receive an almost uninterrupted flow of oil. Meanwhile, Japan attempted to retain its neutral position by continuing to support U.N. Security Council Resolution 242, which called for Israeli withdrawal from occupied Arab lands.

How is it possible that these few desert Arab nations could force such widespread adherence to their policies from the Western nations and Japan? To answer this critical question, let us resort to what might be called a "technical description" of oil consumption in the industrialized West.

In the fall of 1973, Arab nations were producing 19.1 million barrels of oil per day. The United States then consumed about 17.2 million barrels per day, and depended upon Arab exports for about ten percent of this total. Europe consumed fifteen million barrels per day and depended on Arab sources for about sixty-five percent. Japan used 5.2 million barrels per day, of which fifty percent came from the Arab countries.[25] Global dependency on Arab oil had increased from thirty-four percent in 1957 to fifty-four percent in 1973.[26]

It is also necesssary to consider the impact on prices of this heavy world dependency, as OAPEC put their petrodiplomacy into effect. Prices were raised in three steps during the embargo. Prior to the outbreak of the Yom Kippur War on October 6, 1973, the Saudi government's revenue per barrel of oil was about $1.90; when the embargo was finally lifted on March 18, 1974, that revenue had risen to $9.25.[27]

The first price increase, on October 16, 1973, was relatively uninfluenced by the embargo, since the decision had been made prior to that date. The six largest oil-producing countries on the Persian Gulf—Iran, Iraq, Saudi Arabia, Kuwait, the United Arab Emirates, and Qatar—announced a price increase from $3.01 a barrel on October 1 to $5.12 on October 16. The next increase by these nations came on

December 23, effective New Year's Day, when the price per barrel was raised to $11.65. But actual open market prices rose to between fifteen and seventeen dollars per barrel,[28] spearheaded by Libya and Nigeria, who set their new tax reference prices in the range of $14.60 to $18.75 a barrel.

Speaking for the oil producers, the Shah of Iran, arguing that the posted prices of oil should be adjusted upward to reflect market prices (the posted price or tax reference price is, in practice, about forty percent higher than market price), wanted "to junk the current pricing system devised by the international oil companies and base future prices on the costs of supplying alternate sources of energy."[29] Libya and Algeria wanted to push prices as high as possible. In this mini-price war, Iran, Libya, and Algeria were opposed by Saudi Arabia, which proposed smaller increases "to keep the politically motivated embargo separate from OPEC's pricing policy, to avoid the impression that the embargo had been imposed for monetary reasons."[30] Saudi Arabia felt that a sharper increase in price would weaken the political message the Arabs had hoped to communicate to the world.

The next increase occurred in January 1974, when Kuwait announced a sixty percent participation formula, with the price of oil rising by more than one dollar per barrel. These increases in price were rationally based, said the oil producers, considering worldwide inflation rates. Of course, inflation did not suddenly occur with the onset of the Yom Kippur War; it had started long before. Taking advantage of the situation, Iran, in conjunction with the other leading oil producers of the region, spearheaded the move to quadruple oil prices. As one researcher in the petroleum industry noted, "In the absence of the October War and the resulting Arab oil embargo, prices would not have risen so rapidly in so short a period."[31]

The establishment of petroleum pricing levels is a confusing process which developed haphazardly over the last five decades. At its base is the posted price, the point of reference for tax and royalty collection, and buy-back price realization. The royalty was a fixed percentage of the posted price paid by the oil companies to the host countries for extraction of oil. After the royalty was paid and the cost of production was deducted from the posted price, taxes were realized. The buy-back price, usually a percentage of the posted price, was introduced after the oil embargo, when some of the producing countries acquired sixty percent ownership in the oil companies.[32]

Often, the oil-producing countries increase taxes, royalties, or buy-back prices while simultaneously claiming that they are not really raising the price of oil. The production companies, which have not been willing to reduce exorbitant profits, pass the increases along to their customers.

Some readjustments were made by Saudi Arabia, the United Arab Emirates, and Qatar. They reduced their posted prices by forty cents a barrel, but raised the tax, royalty, and buy-back prices slightly, making them almost equal to forty cents. As a result, there was virtually no observable impact on the market, and consumers continued to pay higher prices just as before.

At the end of 1973, the Arabs launched a vigorous publicity campaign to explain their new oil policy to the Western world, holding news conferences and issuing press releases to "clarify" the pan-Arab stand on the use of oil in their struggle for the liberation of Israeli-occupied territories.

At the beginning of 1974, full-page advertisements appeared in both the *Washington Post* and the *New York Times*. The Saudi minister of state for foreign affairs wished the American people a Happy New Year on behalf of the Arab people. Acknowledging the fact that the American "holiday season may have been marred by the hardships of the energy crisis,"[33] the Saudi minister brought home to the Americans the plight of the Arabs by stating, "Ours is haunted by the threat of death and continued aggression."[34]

Referring directly to the embargo, he continued:

> We cut oil supplies to the United States after the United States, which had repeatedly assured us of our rights to our lands, made massive arms deliveries to the Israelis to help them remain in our lands. We did so not to impose a change in U.S. policy in the Middle East, but to demand the implementation of U.S. policy in the Middle East, as it has been repeatedly defined. We did so not to "blackmail" the American people, but to put our case to them as effectively as we knew how.[35]

Almost simultaneously, King Faisal, in his first public speech since the October War, called upon all Muslims to mobilize their resources "to rescue our sacred places in Jerusalem from the Zionist and Communist menaces."[36] Speaking to a group of high-ranking foreign pilgrims, the king, as official protector of Islam's holy sites, told them that he had a special responsibility for liberating Jerusalem, which includes the Al-Aqsa mosque, Islam's third holiest site behind Mecca and Medina.

The worldwide psychological war to justify their use of oil in the Middle East conflict only proved how vulnerable the Arabs themselves really were, for it created an anti-Arab backlash that was ultimately helpful to the Israeli cause. There was much public sympathy for Israel in many European countries, but government policy there called for refraining from any actions that might antagonize the Arabs, lest the oil supply to Europe be endangered. Considering the neutral attitude of the Western European governments and Japan, the Arab oil states decided to end their monthly production cuts and ease restrictions on oil exports to those nations.[37] In an editorial, the *New York Times* said:

> The Arabs have brought their oil weapon into play in the Mideast war, but cautiously and in a manner that leaves the way open for diplomatic cooperation....It is evident from the conduct of the Arab diplomatic delegation...that the leading oil states are more interested in accommodation than in confrontation with the West....[38]

Saudi Arabia, which had taken the lead in imposing the embargo, began to plead for moderation soon thereafter, and it was under the guidance of Oil Minister

Sheikh Yamani that OAPEC, meeting in Vienna, lifted the embargo on March 18, 1974. He also "steered OPEC toward a freezing of crude oil posted prices for another three months...."[39] Oil shipments to the United States were resumed. Yamani forced OPEC to accept a three-month price freeze by threatening to break its united price front and flooding the market with cheap oil. To maintain its unity, OPEC—an extremely successful international cartel—had to agree to Yamani's proposal.[40]

At two OPEC meetings in the summer of 1974—one in Quito, Ecuador in June, and the other in Vienna in September—Yamani again tried to stave off price increases by threatening to increase production. He did so because the Saudi government felt that the price of oil was already substantially high and that any further increase would attract alternative energy substitutes, thereby rendering the Saudi's huge oil reserves useless. Other producers disagreed with Saudi Arabia, and the result was a compromise, with the price being raised slightly.

However, the notion that Saudi Arabia, the largest exporter of oil, could unilaterally bring down oil prices is somewhat misleading:

> An increase in export capacity by 2.5-3.5 million barrels per day, which is all the country would be physically capable of in the next three years, could be largely offset by corresponding reductions in countries with surplus oil revenues.[41]

Nevertheless, temporarily, the oil embargo proved to be the strongest of diplomatic weapons. "It prodded the United States, which in turn prodded Israel, and the result was the disengagement of Israeli and Egyptian forces along the Suez Canal."[42] Although the Soviet Union, the principal arms supplier to the Arabs as well as their chief political ally, called upon the Arab oil producers to maintain the embargo,[43] the Egyptians and the Saudis were eager to reward U.S. Secretary of State Henry Kissinger for his step-by-step shuttle diplomacy to bring about a ceasefire, and the subsequent withdrawal of Israeli troops from the west bank of the Suez Canal.

Many people were puzzled by the Arabs' decision to use a primary commodity such as oil as a weapon in their struggle against Israel because, on the surface, it appeared unfriendly to every one. Initially, at any rate, the use of petroleum was a political act, not an economic one, although some OAPEC and OPEC nations did take advantage of the industrialized world's obvious discomfiture.

The Arab Strategy

Soon after the lifting of the embargo, in April 1974 the Arabs expounded their philosophy at a special session of the United Nations General Assembly. Inaugurating the session, Algerian President Houari Boumediene, who had convened it, developed a "work program in five points" that summarized the Algerian viewpoint on the role of oil in the economic development of the oil-producing countries. The five-point program, which included the nationalization of oil and other resources in the developing countries, was announced by Boumediene after the price hikes of wheat and fertilizers, which had been doubled between June 1972 and September 1973, were rescinded. Reacting to Western criticism of the oil price hike, Boumediene rebutted:

> ...the fundamental difference that explains the greatly dissimilar reactions caused by rises in fertilizer and wheat prices on the one hand, and in the price of oil on the other, resides in the fact that the proceeds of the increase went to developed countries in the first case and to developing countries in the second....[44]

Addressing the special session, Saudi Oil Minister Yamani declared that the oil-exporting nations would reject any attempt to impose outside control on oil prices. He said that Saudi Arabia could afford to cut its oil production by half to raise the price further, but did not do so because of its "sense of responsibility toward the rest of the world."[45] In exchange for this sign of good will, he hoped the industrialized world would help set up a system of diversified industrial structures in Saudi Arabia to assure the Saudis an eventual source of income when oil finally ran out.

The Arab strategy since the embargo had been to divide America and its Atlantic partners, the major consumers of Arab oil. While the United States was firm in its Mideast policy, the Europeans, on the other hand, were not in a position to offer effective resistance to Arab pressure, simply due to their greater dependence on Arab oil. Ironically, Arab pressure on Europe worked almost as a reversal of earlier European colonial policies. Although no permanent dent was created in America's relations with the Benelux states, the tendency in Europe "was not to blame the Arabs, or even Israel, but to say that it was United States' Middle Eastern policy that was causing Europe to freeze this winter."[46] Indirectly, the Europeans were putting pressure on the United States to adopt an "even-handed" policy in the Middle East. Through continued dialogue and closer relations with Western Europe, the Arabs hope to weaken Israel's ties with the industrialized West and particularly with the United States, its chief benefactor. If the Arabs succeed in this strategy, they would win a struggle which has otherwise had no resolution through four wars and countless minor skirmishes.

Another Arab strategy has been to isolate Israel from the mainstream of world politics, and thus to create a sense of insecurity for the Jewish state. The need for peace is greater for Israel than for the Arabs, both economically and politically, principally because of three developments that occurred following the 1973 war. The fear of insecurity had slowed immigration to Israel, and emigration from the Jewish state to other countries was accelerating. Added to this is the still very high inflation rate in Israel due to abnormally high military spending; this resulted in a devaluation of the Israeli pound by forty-three percent in 1974 and again by two percent in 1975, with monthly two percent devaluations slated if the economy continues to decline. At the same time, foreign investment in Israel in 1975 slumped by about sixty percent.[47] Fear of an Arab boycott is seen as a factor inhibiting all foreign investments in Israel. Politically, therefore, the Arabs were effective in isolating Israel internationally. Following the October War, many Afro-Asian nations, which had earlier established diplomatic ties with Israel, severed those relations. Thus, Israel became increasingly insecure, while the Arabs acquired tremendous wealth in the form of petrodollars. As the Palestinians gained more sympathy in the world, there was a commensurate reduction in support for Israel, which was perceived as an aggressor state. This image reached its peak with the Israeli incursion into Lebanon. The Arabs were also successful in cutting off support for Israel by the U.N. Educational, Scientific, and Cultural Organization (UNESCO) in 1974. In the future, the Arabs might initiate additional actions by the U.N. and other such specialized international agencies:

> It can be said that Israel is, in many respects, alone in the world because its own orientation is against the general trend. Even American-Israeli relations are in the process of change, owing largely to the fact that the United States can no longer centre its Middle Eastern policies on the interests of Zionism alone.[48]

If the deliberate physical and psychological isolation of Israel from its neighbors and from much of the outside world continues, and the Arabs continue to gain in power, prestige, and credibility, it is likely that the Israeli position will generally continue to erode in the 1990s.

What was an energy crisis for the industrialized world was a tremendous political and economic success for the oil-producing world. The initial Arab military victories in the October War and their use of oil as a weapon showed that they were learning not only the tactics of modern warfare, but also developing their diplomatic skills. The moderate position has been under constant pressure from those in the Mideast who feel that only militancy pays.[49] It was for this reason that Saudi Arabia shunned its policy of moderation and began to use its oil as a weapon in the Mideast conflict; it could not afford to be seen as the most reluctant state to satisfy the nationalist aspirations of Arabs. At the same time, Saudi Arabia and other nations realized that their oil sword was a "double-edged weapon,"[50] according to President Habib Bourguiba of Tunisia, an oil-less Arab state in North Africa. Before the embargo could cause irreparable damage to the American economy (which would, in turn, directly affect Arab economic interests), it was lifted. As one Arab minister maintained:

> If the embargo were to remain, we would see a major recession in America. That, in turn, would affect all of us adversely. Our economies, our regimes, our very survival depend on a healthy United States economy.[51]

The early lifting of the embargo indicated that the Arabs, particularly the Saudis, had decided not to abuse their economic power. "There is a growing real-

49

ization that this power—based on hydrocarbons—is finite and that alternative sources of revenue should be developed speedily."[52] According to some indications, Saudi Arabia's oil reserves will last until the year 2039, at which time the desert kingdom will find itself without resources, unless oil revenues are wisely invested.[53]

Saudi Arabia's petroleum was developed exclusively by American companies. The Saudis need U.S. technology to create a functional economic infrastructure on which their future oil-less economy can be based. This is a gigantic undertaking which can only be provided by the industrialized West in a massive transfer of resources, i.e., a trade-off of oil for knowledge.

Paradoxically, the oil embargo strengthened the U.S. position in the Middle East, especially in Saudi Arabia. Saudi relations with American oil companies have undergone many changes since the beginning of their operations in the 1930s, but it is noteworthy that, although the principal object of the oil embargo was to isolate the United States and, through it, Israel, American oil companies have continued to operate in Saudi Arabia.

The onslaught of the energy crisis, and the increasing dependence of the world on Middle Eastern oil, have made oil a controversial issue, and have created a climate full of doubt and suspicion regarding the motives of the host governments and their relations with the oil companies, as well as the companies' relations with their own countries.

A Palestinian-Israeli Issue

The oil embargo was established not to effect a cease-fire in the October War, but to seek explicitly the evacuation of Israeli forces from all Arab lands occupied during the June War of 1967. This indicated that the Arabs were willing to accommodate Israel within the original boundaries established by the United Nations in 1948. Another reason for the oil embargo was to restore the rights of the Palestinians. Although this was not spelled out during the October War, such restoration would inevitably mean the return to an independent Palestine, which, in turn, implied its separation from Israeli occupied lands.

The Arab states claim that the Arab-Israeli conflict is essentially a Palestinian-Israeli issue, based on the fact that the Palestinians were driven from their homes in 1948 and now live as second-class refugees throughout the Arab world. Although Arabs, they prefer to be known as Palestinians due to nostalgic feelings toward a homeland many have never seen.

The Palestinian movement was dramatized at the Rabat Summit in October 1974, when the Palestinian Liberation Organization (PLO) won a major diplomatic victory by convincing twenty Arab nations to support its claim as the sole representative of the Palestinian people, despite the opposition of Jordan's King Hussein, who had formerly ruled some of those areas. He was forced to succumb to the unanimous pressure of the Arab world.

The United Nations, which in effect created the situation through its 1947 resolution establishing the state of Israel, bent tradition by inviting the head of the PLO, a political movement, to address the General Assembly as though he represented a formal government.[54]

Yasser Arafat, in his speech before the U.N. General Assembly on November 13, 1974, took an all-or-nothing approach; this prompted passage on November 22 of a General Assembly resolution recognizing the rights of the Palestinians to independence and sovereignty in Palestine.[55] It passed by a vote of eighty-nine to eight, with thirty-seven abstentions, mostly by European and Latin American countries. The United States, Israel, Norway, Iceland, Bolivia, Chile, Costa Rica, and Nicaragua voted "no."[56]

Of all the developments in the Middle East since the creation of the state of Israel, the passage of the Palestinian resolution was the most significant. In its most simplistic sense, Palestine had achieved official recognition from the same world body that had created Israel. What remains to be seen is whether the resolution will actually have any visible results. The original United Nations resolution of 1947 partitioned British-controlled Palestine into Jewish, Arab, and international sectors. The Jews were given fifty-six percent of the territory, the Arabs forty-two percent, and the remaining two percent in Jerusalem was made an international zone open to all parties. Israel eventually took over all of Palestine as a result of a series of conflicts initially started by both the surrounding Arab states and by the Palestinian Arabs themselves. The resulting morass seems at times unsolvable.

Aftermath

The use of oil as a weapon of diplomacy strengthened the hand of the Palestinians. They received an unexpected boost when the late Shah of Iran, who had shown new support for the Arabs, joined President Anwar Sadat in calling for Israel's total withdrawal from all occupied Arab lands, thereby affirming the right of the Palestinian people to their homeland.[57]

As time passed, the effect of Arab petrodiplomacy was felt more in the international economic arena than in the political one, a direct result of the escalation of oil prices. Although Saudi Arabia led the Arab nations in imposing the embargo, probably there was no intention initially of increasing prices to such a high level. Nevertheless, once the situation mushroomed out of control, both Iran and Venezuela took the lead in increasing prices. The quadrupling of oil prices in little more than a year was perceived as the immediate cause of economic chaos throughout the world, although this was by no means the only reason for these developments. Still, the sudden large increase did precipitate a worldwide recession that for a short time threatened to slide into global depression. Such a disruption in the world economic structure would ultimately have harmed the Arabs as much as anyone else, a fact which the cooler heads among them quite clearly perceived.

The growing disparity between oil haves and have-nots has resulted in widespread international financial chaos and misunderstanding. The inequities have been accentuated by the fact that much of the international oil supply is now controlled by a handful of developing Third World nations that are still relatively poor when compared to their Western brothers. Naturally, they have jealously guarded their new-found wealth against encroachment from the outside. But not all jealousies or conflicts are amenable to quick solutions. A return to the old order is impossible. A major transfer of financial resources and the power that goes with it has begun, and the world has already adjusted to the "new reality," as the Arabs call it. The danger of extremism still remains, as does the possibility of a new oil embargo and a subsequent explosion in oil prices.

Before the war broke out between the Western coalition headed by the United States and Iraq on January 16, 1991, some experts believed the oil market could briefly bid the price of oil as high as $100 per barrel. Instead, the price fell the day after the first U.S. and Allied attack.

The abrupt swings in oil prices of the first half of 1991 are a sharp contrast to a few years ago, when the price of oil was stable for months or years at a time and controlled by OPEC—two of many ways the existence of the new oil market has made this crisis different from the two energy crises of the 1973-74 and 1978-79.

There is no hidden or controlled oil market; world oil is now sold in free market competition. The new oil market actually is two markets: the traditional unregulated "spot" or "cash" market in oil and petroleum products, a worldwide bazaar in which oil producers, refiners, and users barter privately among themselves for supplies for immediate or future delivery; and the regulated "futures" market, in the frenetic trading pits of the stock exhange, in which the arcane practice of buying and selling agricultural commodities for future delivery at a guaranteed price has been adapted to the oil business.

By playing these two markets off against each other, traders seek possible deals for their clients, buying what amounts to insurance, or "hedging," against future price fluctuations, and wringing opportunistic profits from wrinkles in the market.

For the oil companies, it is a political and public relations problem of the first magnitude. During the 1991 war amid the oil fields of the Persian Gulf, demonstrators carried picket signs saying "No Blood for Oil," and gasoline prices did not seem to tumble as quickly as the price of crude oil did. Most of the major oil companies had sharp profit increases in the fourth quarter of 1990 (October-December). Stock analysts maintained that profits were getting a boost from higher crude prices, which averaged $32.20 per barrel in the fourth quarter of 1989. The higher prices were caused by the crisis in the Persian Gulf, although prices fell after hostilities broke.

IV.

AMERICAN PEACE INITIATIVES

The importance of achieving a comprehensive peace settlement in the Middle East cannot be exaggerated. The Arab-Israeli wars, the Iran-Iraq wars, and the more recent Gulf War between the international coalition led by the United States and Iraq are constant reminders of the volatility of the region. Escalation of these wars could easily jeopardize the flow of oil from the Persian Gulf and draw the United States into a dangerous military confrontation with the Soviet Union. The consequences of such a confrontation would be devastating for the Middle East, if not for the entire world.

In this section, we will examine U.S. attempts to promote a permanent, negotiated peace in the Middle East, leading to the Camp David Summit and the subsequent Egyptian-Israeli peace treaty. American efforts to achieve a settlement of Arab-Israeli differences have historically fallen short of their goal. Thus the Egyptian-Israeli peace treaty looms ever larger as the first major breakthrough in what was perceived by the West as an inpenetrable Arab intransigence.

Traditionally, American policy in the Middle East centered directly on containing the Soviet Union's influence, through maintaining political stability and peace in the region. Instability (i.e., war) was considered conducive to the growth of Soviet influence. Another major U.S. policy interest was its support of Israel. As détente was achieved for a time between the superpowers, American policy in the Middle East began to change. "Containment and fear of a monolithic communism have outlived their utility. The Dulles-devised regional security pacts of the fifties are remnants of a polarization that is giving way to pluralism."[1] Current U.S. policy is based on gaining the friendship of as many nations as possible in the region while simultaneously ensuring Israel's security. Of these two major principles, the second was often paramount, to a point where the Israelis, Soviets, Americans, and Arabs have all come to identify the United States with the Israeli cause.

At the beginning of the twentieth century, American interests in the Middle East were limited by the British presence there. With the British attempt to monopolize the vast oil reserves of the Middle East through U.N. mandates, U.S. involvement in Middle Eastern affairs heightened. America's justification for claiming a share of Arabian oil resources was based on the fact that it had supplied the Allied powers during both world wars with vast amounts of American oil. The establishment of the Turkish Petroleum Company in 1928, which included several U.S. companies as backers, was the beginning of American economic involvement in the region. Although limited at the time, America's investment in Middle East-

53

ern oil grew as the use of petroleum in the United States increased after 1945.

Following the end of World War II, Soviet pressures on Iran, Turkey, and Greece increased, and the United States assumed the role of their protector against communism. The Truman Doctrine set the tone of U.S. policy in the Middle East. As President Truman said, "Totalitarian regimes imposed on free people, by indirect or direct aggression, undermine the foundations of international peace and hence the security of the U.S."[2]

The most important development in U.S. policy *vis-à-vis* Israel took place in 1947, when the American government supported the United Nations General Assembly resolution creating the state of Israel. As a result of this vote, and America's subsequent recognition of Israel in 1948, the U.S. became directly involved in the Arab-Israeli conflicts which followed. Support for Israel grew as the horrors of the Holocaust became better known to the world, partly as the result of well-organized Jewish lobbying efforts in the United States.

Superpower Interests

While Arab-Israeli conflicts have their own causes and characters, they are interrelated when they involve the interests of the two superpowers. The stated Soviet policy on Israel is not aimed at the destruction of that state, but to force it to relinquish its territorial gains. This was the philosophy behind U.N. Security Council Resolution 242, which both Washington and Moscow helped to draft and which was adopted on November 22, 1967. At one point during the fourth Arab-Israeli war, the two superpowers were on the verge of armed conflict in the Middle East, but, thanks to the famous shuttle diplomacy of Secretary of State Kissinger, a dangerous confrontation was avoided. In the words of Harvard University Professor Nadav Safran:

> Besides defusing an explosive situation, starting off a process of negotiation for the first time in 25 years, setting up hopeful precedents for compromise, and beginning to generate mutual trust between the antagonists, the disengagement agreements involved a substantial modification of past patterns of inter-Arab politics.[3]

Another key Security Council action on the subject was Resolution 338 (adopted October 22, 1973). Taken together, these resolutions require the parties to negotiate peace agreements "concurrently" with security arrangements. According to the interpretation of Eugene V. Rostow, former U.S. undersecretary of state, "Under the Security Council resolutions, Israel is not required to withdraw one inch from the territories it holds as the occupying power until its Arab neighbors have made peace."[4]

Following the end of war in 1973, both radical and moderate leaders in the Arab world began cooperating with the United States to reach disengagement agreements. This sudden *rapprochement* elevated the U.S. into a position of trust and influence in much of the Arab world.[5] The elements that made this change in Arab attitudes possible extend further than the disengagement agreements. Again, in the words of Safran:

> They include strong shared interests with the United States on the part of conservative Arab countries, beneath their expressed resentment of American policy toward Israel; strong resentment on the part of radical Arab countries toward the Soviet Union, beneath their cooperation with it; fears on the part of both radical and conservative Arab countries about the costs and outcome of continuing confrontation and war; and hopes on the part of the Arabs that American behavior in the last stage of the October War, which saved them from the humiliation of another defeat, portended a favorable change in American policy.[6]

Kissinger's attempt through shuttle diplomacy to nudge the Mideast disputants toward a step-by-step settlement received a major setback following the Arab summit at Rabat, which strengthened the role of the PLO. The situation was further complicated by the oil-rich nations of the region who were each engaged in huge rearmament programs, and were also supporting the PLO fighters with funds and matériel. According to George W. Ball, former U.S. undersecretary of state:

> One lesson we should have learned from the experience of past months is that highly personalized diplomacy is effective only in a bilateral setting; it has limited value in a complex situation involving many countries. Thus, the attempt to settle the Arab-Israeli issue by shutting out both the more activist Arab states and the Soviet Union was predestined to failure.[7]

From the beginning of Kissinger's efforts, it was clear that his approach was pragmatic and not legalistic; however, it was not as clear precisely how he thought he could secure an Israeli withdrawal within the boundaries that existed before 1967. Ball, among others, believes this could only have been accomplished "in the multilateral setting of the Geneva Conference, with participation of all the principal Arab states, including the most radical, and with the Soviets acting as cochairmen."[8]

The implicit assumption that Israel would be required to return to its 1967 frontiers, with only slightly modified borders, seemed on its surface wholly unacceptable to Israel. But "Kissinger was understood to feel that if the United States were ready to press for a full Israeli pullback, there would be no need for Soviet cooperation in the process."[9] Kissinger's shuttle diplomacy was undertaken merely to keep the momentum of negotiations moving. However, the momentum stopped because of intransigence on both sides, and his overall strategy came to nought largely because of the changing role of the PLO, and its subsequent influence in Arab affairs. The Arab states were put in the position of either supporting the legitimacy of

PLO aspirations, or being labelled as traitors to the Arab cause. Kissinger's failure to promote some sort of dialogue between Jordan and Israel, in advance of the Rabat summit, was a major opportunity missed. Previously, the Arab nations had demanded the destruction of the state of Israel; while this stand was now modified, they still demanded that Israel withdraw from the territories it had occupied in 1967 and 1973. PLO leader Arafat reaffirmed before the U.N. General Assembly in November 1974 that the creation of a secular Palestinian state in Palestine, which includes Israel proper, was the goal toward which most Palestinians were striving. To date, he said, the Arabs had fought the Palestinians' wars; now, the Palestinians themselves would take a leading role in the attempt to liberate their homeland from Israeli occupation. It was precisely for this reason that the PLO was given sole responsibility at Rabat to speak and act for the Palestinians.

From the beginning of his personal crusade, Kissinger was warned by many analysts of the crippling contradictions inherent in his policy. He repeatedly tried to convince Egyptian President Sadat of the merits of his approach to peace in the Middle East, despite the Syrians and the Palestinians denouncing the move. The Sadat-Kissinger understanding was based on their joint conviction that once Israeli forces pulled back from the strategic Mitla and Giddi mountain passes in the Sinai, as well as from the Abu Rudeis oil fields at the peninsula's southeastern edge, peace mediation efforts on other fronts could be then undertaken at the Geneva Conference. Israel agreed to the return of these territories and the oil fields in exchange for a declaration of non-belligerency from Egypt. President Sadat was unwilling to make such a declaration directly, but gave explicit assurances that if two hundred American civilian technicians were stationed at early-warning stations on the peninsula, he would pledge not to use force. The Egyptians were ready to bear the military and economic costs of non-belligerency, but Israel wanted a categorical public declaration. Israeli intransigence was based on the ancient concept that war is a legal means of acquiring territory, and such conquests should not be returned without a declaration of political non-belligerency. Egypt could probably have agreed to such a declaration if all Arab territories occupied by Israel were returned at the same time. The Egyptian attitude was that such a declaration would be tantamount to admitting the illegality of its war with Israel, while the latter could still retain most of the occupied lands. Egypt also would have consented to the legitimization of the Israeli occupation of the Jordanian and Syrian territories.

Sadat knew that once Egypt agreed to an interim settlement with Israel, that deep divisions would be aroused in the Arab world. Centrifugal forces would reemerge in Arab politics, and Palestinian activists might resort to violence on a larger scale. As soon as the news of the last round of Kissinger's initiative became public, the Palestinians openly challenged Sadat. President Assad of Syria, fearful that a separate Egyptian settlement with Israel might diminish his prospects of regaining the Golan Heights through peaceful means, created a united political and military command with the PLO.

Needless to say, a lasting peace in the Middle East, argues the PLO, depends on a complete Israeli withdrawal from all occupied Arab territories, including the Gaza Strip, the Golan Heights, and the West Bank. Israel insists that it must retain the Golan Heights and the Nahal outposts along the Jordan River for security reasons. Israeli annexation of Jerusalem poses another seemingly insoluble problem, for what is a security problem for Israel is equally a security issue for the Arabs.

Prospects for Peace

Under the above conditions, what are the prospects of a peaceful settlement? One hope is the reconvention of the Geneva Conference under the auspices of the United Nations, the United States, and the Soviet Union, in which the Arab nations, Israel, and the Palestinians would attempt to work out their differences. The planning and organization of a conference of so many diverse elements, involving issues as complex as Israel's borders and the question of a Palestinian state, is such that no quick decision can be expected. Even assuming that such a conference resumed in Geneva, endless debates would certainly build pressure for Israel to withdraw its forces from all occupied Arab territories. The U.S. attitude must be one of evenhandedness in the Mideast. We have already seen certain U.S. senators and congressmen becoming more discriminating and reserved in their attitudes toward Israel; even President Gerald Ford and Secretary Kissinger complained of Israeli intransigence and inflexibility.[10] Ford also ordered a formal review of American policy in the Mideast after the 1973 war. The White House announcement came after the collapse of the tenth round of Kissinger's shuttle diplomacy, when the world was beginning to blame Israel for its uncompromising attitude. Ford's order was undoubtedly calculated to prevent the cooling of otherwise warm American relations with such moderate Arab states as Egypt and Saudi Arabia. But nothing spectacular occurred as the result of America's reassessment of its Middle Eastern policies. However, Jewish influence on U.S. foreign policy is clearly not as strong as it once was, having been offset to some degree by those members of the business world favoring contact with the Arabs. Israel's problem lies with the White House rather than with the Congress, where Israeli support has continued almost unabated. Israeli strategy has been to stand firm, maintain its lobbying activities, and wait for a reassessment of U.S. policy toward the Mideast, on the assumption that the White House cannot ignore Israeli requests for military and economic assistance.

America's Special Relationship with Israel

President Jimmy Carter reaffirmed American relations with Israel at a press conference on May 13, 1977, when he said:

> We have a special relationship with Israel. It's absolutely crucial that no one in our country or around the world ever doubt that our number one commitment in the Middle East is to protect the right of Israel to exist, to exist permanently, and to exist in peace. It's a special relationship.[11]

As a result of this relationship, the United States has been walking a diplomatic tightrope in the Mideast for the last four decades. Tenuous relationships with Arab states, America's need for Arab oil, Third World political support for the PLO, and the constant threat of Soviet penetration into the area, have all contributed to an urgent American desire for a permanent peace settlement in the Middle East.

Carter's strong, pre-election commitment to Israel gave way to a more moderate stance at the urging of the Departments of State, Energy, and Defense. The Arab oil weapon was probably uppermost in Carter's policy considerations. Carter became the first American head of state to discuss the concept of a "Palestinian homeland,"[12] recognizing the Palestinian problem as the core issue in the Arab-Israeli dispute, at least from the Arab point of view.

The ambiguity of Carter's position on the Palestinian question added to the confusion and uncertainty of the peace efforts, and a final settlement between the Arabs and the Israelis was considered impossible. Instead, a joint United States-Soviet statement called for a Geneva Conference no later than December 1977 to work out a comprehensive and lasting solution to the conflict.[13] But the response from all parties was negative. Egypt and Israel objected to Soviet participation in the negotiations. Most of the other Arab nations objected to direct negotiations with Israel. The inclusion of a delegation from the PLO was viewed with alarm by Israel and its American supporters.

While the impasse continued, a dramatic development in Arab-Israeli politics took place: President Sadat stunned the world by visiting Israel, ostensibly to remove the psychological barriers which had separated the Arabs and Israelis for so many years. The Sadat visit served to shift the focus of the peace initiative from a multilateral to a bilateral one. President Carter sought to capitalize on this development and especially on the new attitude of President Sadat. The latter addressed the Israeli Knesset and outlined five principles of a possible peace settlement. The hard-line Arab states condemned his actions, while moderate Arab nations maintained a low profile.

Subsequently, Egyptian and Israeli officials met in Cairo to discuss further details concerning the peace process, followed by Israeli Prime Minister Menachem Begin's visit to Washington, where he presented his proposals for peace to President Carter. Begin's plan, calling for Israeli relinquishment of the Sinai and limited self-rule for the West Bank and Gaza Strip, in exchange for normalized relations with the Carter administration, although optimistic, evoked only a guarded response.

In late December of 1977, a meeting between Sadat and Begin was held at Ismailia, Egypt. The talks failed over the question of autonomy for the West Bank. Further talks also resulted in a stalemate, and Sadat stated that there was no hope of reaching a settlement.[14] Both sides stood firm on their proposals and began to criticize each other. Relations between the parties again began to deteriorate, following an age-old pattern.

The Camp David Accord

President Carter became concerned that the impasse would jeopardize the fragile relations developing between Egypt and Israel and, with it, destroy any chance for peace in the Middle East. In the biggest risk he took as president, Carter invited the two leaders to Camp David for face-to-face talks aimed at breaking the stalemate. The announcement of the summit came at a time when Carter's popularity was at its lowest point. Both Sadat and Begin were under pressure not to deviate from their previously stated positions, and the prospects for compromise were dim.

In thirteen days of arduous negotiations, initiated in an atmosphere of gloom and mutual suspicion, Carter convinced the two leaders to accept two agreements that broke new ground. Essentially, the accords were agreements to agree, rather than an actual settlement of the difficult issues dividing the two nations: the two agreements dealt with the Sinai Peninsula and a framework for settling the future of the West Bank and Gaza Strip.[15]

The negotiations proved to be difficult and time consuming. The December 17 deadline specified in the agreement soon passed, and hopes of ratification faded. The Arab nations pressured Sadat not to accept a peace treaty with Israel at the expense of the rights of the Palestinians. Begin's position, as leader of a fractious coalition government, was a great handicap, both to him and the others.

An American attempt to break the impasse through Secretary of State Cyrus Vance's shuttle diplomacy failed. The Carter administration then submitted a compromise proposal. On March 15, 1979, the Egyptian cabinet voted unanimously to approve the draft peace treaty. The Israeli cabinet approved it on March 21, and the treaty was formally signed in Washington on March 26 by Sadat and Begin, with President Carter as witness.

Under the agreement, Egypt and Israel were required to implement the framework established at Camp David in September of 1978. A timetable was established for carrying out the provisions of the treaty. Within three years, the final withdrawal of Israeli forces and civilian settlements from the Sinai would complete the timetable. On April 25, 1982, this was actually realized.

The above chronology of events leading to the final agreement is ample proof of the difficulties involved. There is no doubt that President Carter's personal commitment and prestige were important factors in the success of the negotiations. The threat of future Arab-Israeli wars has been much reduced as a result—without Egypt, the other Arab states are unable to wage a successful war against Israel.

The extent to which the Arab use of oil as a political weapon precipitated the peace initiative is unclear. Certainly, the original embargo imposed during the Yom Kippur War shocked the U.S. out of its complacency, and helped spur America to work for a permanent, stabilizing settlement. As promised to the Arab leaders, the United States government arranged a cease-fire and the initial withdrawal of Israeli troops from the Suez Canal and part of the Golan Heights.

Some observers have argued that the signing of the Camp David Accord was only minimally dependent on the oil embargo, since the latter had been lifted some five years previously. The U.S. desire to create a *rapprochement* between Israel and its Arab neighbors was perhaps due more to American attempts to prevent Soviet inroads in the region.

The Camp David formula left open for future negotiations the settlement of the Palestinian question and the future of the West Bank, the Golan Heights, and the Gaza Strip. Still, it is unlikely that the accord will lead to a tangible diplomatic solution to these problems in the near future. Indeed, Egyptian President Hosni Mubarak has been forced to cool relations with Israel in order to reestablish ties with friendly Arab states, and to appease Muslim radicals which threaten his rule.

Achieving a permanent peace settlement in the Middle East acceptable to all parties involved is an extremely difficult task. Camp David was an excellent beginning, but the momentum of Camp David is now lost. It can be revived only if the Arabs and the Israelis truly want to avoid future bloodshed and achieve territorial readjustments without war.

Window of Opportunity

As the Persian Gulf War ended on February 27, 1991, the potential for war in the short term in the Middle East had been reduced. But the prospects of a future war between the Arabs and Israelis remain great. With this in mind, both President George Bush and Secretary of State James A. Baker III have insisted that a "window of opportunity" has been created for Arab states and Israel to advance toward a comprehensive settlement that has eluded the Middle East for the last four decades.

But in August 1991, as Baker completed his sixth diplomatic mission to the Middle East during the postwar period, it became apparent that if his exhaustive tours have clarified anything, it is that the war brought about, at best, only small changes in the way Arabs and Israelis perceive the regional order and their place in it.

Attempts by Baker to exploit the postwar situation have repeatedly backfired. First, a plan for "confidence-building measures" by the two sides stalled when neither Israeli nor Arab leaders proved willing to initiate the first concession. Then, an attempt by Baker to overcome the thorny problem of launching Israeli-Palestinian talks through a "second track" of Israeli-Arab negotiations only succeeded in creating a second thicket of procedural disputes to be solved.

It is clear that the initial, hopeful phase of postwar U.S. diplomacy has ended. If the peace process continues, it will probably be more modest and seek more limited aims; in effect, it will return to the old ideas and realities with which Baker grappled before Iraq invaded Kuwait.

In retrospect, the very American perception of a "window of opportunity" seems driven as much by political imperatives as by facts. During the war's build-up, as Iraqi President Saddam Hussein appealed to Arab sentiment by repeatedly raising the issue of Israel's occupation of Arab lands, President Bush countered by pledging that the Israeli-Palestinian dispute would be high on the postwar agenda.

In fact, neither Israelis nor Palestinians, embroiled in increasingly bitter conflict during the Gulf crisis, believed the postwar period would open the door to resolving their long struggle. Instead, Israelis hoped the U.S. alliance with Saudi Arabia, Kuwait, and Syria might allow for postwar American pressure on those states to drop their hostility to the Jewish state. The Arabs, conversely, believed that their war-time partnership with the United States would be rewarded with postwar U.S. pressure on Israel.

American officials point out that beyond these self-interested expectations, there were several signs of more fundamental changes in the region. Following decades of superpower rivalry in the Middle East, the Soviet Union appeared eager to cooperate with the United States in an effort for peace, using its substantial influence with Arab leaders and its improving relationship with Israel.

The Bush administration's basic approach was to pressure Israel and the Arab states to consider taking a series of incremental steps toward each other, the thinking behind this being that any large-scale American peace plan would instantly become a target and be attacked in its particulars. So Baker began putting together an approach in which he would attempt to persuade the various players to take small steps toward peace on their own.

In this environment, Israeli military strength, so assiduously cultivated over the decades in the interests of promoting the security of a small and vulnerable state, now seems to thwart the emergence of an Arab-Israeli settlement. Strong enough to deter any combination of regional threats arrayed against it, Israel cannot be pressured to adopt positions or enter into agreements against its wishes. In the absence of compromise by both the Arabs and the Israelis, the *Intifada*, or uprising, in the occupied territories will continue indefinitely and a settlement of the vexing Arab-Israeli conflict will remain a distant vision.

V.

THE IMPACT OF OPEC PETROLISM

Petrolism—whether viewed as a supplement to political, economic, or military weakness, or as a tool for escalating the price of oil—originally inspired OAPEC to use oil for political reasons. This catapulted the parent organization of OPEC into a position of power in the world. Although the Arab-Israeli conflict and the Palestinian issue are of primary importance to the Arab states, it was Iran, a non-Arab state, that was instrumental in persuading them to impose an embargo on supplies in late 1973. In the price war that followed, all other OPEC members joined together united against the consuming nations.

Among the regional organizations that have been founded since World War II, none has attained more prominence than OPEC. Since its formation in 1960, OPEC has successfully dealt with both oil-consuming nations and multinational oil companies. The shift in petropower has been exponential, moving, with brief interludes, away from the industrialized West toward the Middle East. And yet, "although the acronym OPEC is recognized, there has been no concomitant rise in understanding the organization."[1]

The 1960s witnessed several important changes in the world energy configuration. Ignoring the concerns of the exporting nations, the international oil companies lowered oil prices in 1960, the largest price reduction being announced by Exxon: fourteen cents of the posted price. In the decade following the creation of OPEC, the producing-exporting countries were unsuccessful in raising prices to pre-1960 levels, although they were able to prevent any further declines.

Still, while OPEC was powerless to raise prices during the 1960s, it did manage to alter the structure of the world oil market in certain basic ways. The decline of the United States as a producer and discoverer of oil forced it to begin importing OPEC oil to make up the deficit. Consumption continued to increase in all the industrial countries. Meanwhile, the producing-exporting countries were gradually taking over complete control of the oil industry in their own states, and began to coordinate their public policies through OPEC.

OPEC consists of ten Muslim nations and three non-Muslim nations: Saudi Arabia, Kuwait, Libya, Iraq, Algeria, the United Arab Emirates, Qatar, Iran, Nigeria, Indonesia, Venezuela, Ecuador, and Gabon (an associate member).[2] Most are undemocratic countries run by kings, sheikhs, or dictators.

The major contrasting feature of OPEC is the uneven distribution of oil and population among its members. Some of the members have small resources in relation to their populations, while others have large resources and small populations.

The two groups are constantly at odds. Some of them require large incomes but have little potential to increase output, while others require little income, but have a considerable ability to increase production.

This broad spectrum of interests, based upon natural resources, local economic needs, and maldistribution of population within OPEC, provides the basis for serious differences over oil policy. Countries with more abundant reserves tend to be more conservative: Saudi Arabia, Kuwait, and the United Arab Emirates fall into this category. On the other hand, Libya, Algeria, and Iraq, with fewer reserves, often behave radically or even erratically. These states, in contrast to the conservatives, are constantly seeking higher price levels, and are generally more aggressive in their oil policies. The radicals fear quicker exhaustion of their finite resources and wish to develop a sellers' market as early as possible. As a result, constant friction, intrigue, and even war have occurred, and, as we have seen in the Gulf War, will continue to occur.

Significant differences also exist in the countries' political and economic structures, ranging from centrally-planned to private-enterprise economies, with varying degrees of public sector involvement.

In "Is Nigeria OPEC's Graveyard?," *The Economist* reported in 1982 that Nigeria was on the brink of economic collapse.[3] Its central bank reserves had fallen from about ten billion dollars in 1981 to a little over one billion dollars in April 1982, and the government was unable to meet its foreign financial debt obligations. Nigeria was thus forced to curtail importing almost all foreign goods. Saudi Arabia and other OPEC members attempted to assist Nigeria by providing loans.

Nigeria found itself in such a situation because it failed to acknowledge the economic law of supply and demand. It was unable to sell its oil at the relatively high price of $35.50 per barrel, a level which Nigeria required in order to sustain its economic growth. Attempts by Saudi Arabia and other OPEC members to persuade oil companies to buy Nigerian oil failed to generate sales. From the oil companies' perspective, the stakes are billions of dollars in oil revenues. For the producers, the issue may well be the continued existence of OPEC as an effective force in world oil politics.

With such diversities and difficulties, can we truly consider OPEC a cartel? A cartel, in an economic sense, implies the ability of an organization to fix prices by manipulating the rather inflexible laws of supply and demand. But, as on many occasions in the last thirty-one years, OPEC has been unable to agree on basic steps to curtail production when demand is low, or to lower prices when output is high. Writing in the *Wall Street Journal*, a Saudi academic said about OPEC:

> If OPEC is a cartel, it must have developed a system which guarantees that no member produces more than it is supposed to, either by punishing violators or by bribing them through side payments....No such system exists; no such discipline has ever been exercised....What in fact determines the world oil price is the world's total supply of oil and total demand for it. If OPEC affects the price of oil it must either influence demand or supply.

Obviously, it has no influence on the individual countries' rate of oil outputs either.[4]

OPEC oil policy must be viewed from both economic and political perspectives. Economically, OPEC oil prices are determined by the extent to which it can establish a monopolistic control of the market. In political terms, oil exports are the result of policies and decisions made in the context of local, national, regional, and global politics by OPEC's members. The political-economic power that OPEC wielded when it acted in concert did not become evident until the 1973 oil embargo and OPEC's resulting production cutbacks. At the time of the embargo, OPEC provided about eighty-six percent of the non-communist world's oil exports and fifty-five percent of total production. OPEC nations owned two-thirds of the world's proven reserves. The importance of these resources and production grew rapidly in the 1970s as world demand for oil soared. The industrialized world embarked on an oil consumption binge because prices were low, supplies plentiful, and Western economies burgeoning. The U.S. alone consumed about one-third of the total world oil supply.[5]

Although not directly linked to oil, the Arab-Israeli war of 1973 demonstrated the vulnerability of the world to the pressure of petropolitics. The ensuing oil embargo dramatically demonstrated the power of the oil weapon. Both Arab and non-Arab members of OPEC sought to exploit the situation by unilaterally increasing prices.

The embargo was also immensely beneficial to the Arabs from a political point of view. The European Economic Community adopted pro-Arab statements, and Japan switched its neutral stance, appealing to Israel to withdraw from the occupied territories. The United States, too, was influenced by the embargo, which provided the impetus behind U.S. peace-keeping efforts in the Middle East.

The events of 1973 increased the value of OPEC exports in 1974 to eighty billion dollars, ten percent of the total value of world exports that year. This vast increase in earnings generated a huge balance of payments surplus for the OPEC nations, and significant deficits for the industrialized world. Estimates of the magnitude of the cumulative surplus over the five-year period from 1975-80 range from $200 billion to $600 billion, depending upon the sources and the assumptions they have made.[6] On the other side, the 1980 deficits of the industrialized states have been estimated at about fifty billion dollars, and that of the less developed countries (LDCs) at nearly seventy billion dollars. The cumulative foreign debt of the LDCs reached approximately $440 billion in 1981.[7] Currently, the LDCs owe more than $1.2 trillion to the governments and banks of the developed nations.

In the past, both oil companies and consuming nations have guided the policies of the producing states. The oil embargo proved that in the present international climate, "the producing nations have wrested control of their resources and will use them in the determination of their own destinies."[8]

Nevertheless, a gap exists in the perceptions and interests of the OPEC nations and their Western consumers. Although OPEC is investing its revenues in the West, it is doing so for its own reasons, and not in response to warnings from

Western politicians and economists that a possible economic collapse looms large on the horizon. The OPEC nations held about sixty-two billion dollars in investments in U.S. treasury bills and notes in 1981.[9] While the West argues over the need for recycling petrodollars, OPEC policymakers view this claim with suspicion, and generally oppose the concept of recycling. Apparently, OPEC doubts the possible world doom envisaged by the West. Yet the effects of OPEC policies on the consuming countries include skyrocketing inflation and sustained recession, with profound political repercussions. But OPEC members have found their apparent power an uncertain blessing. Their failure to develop pricing formulas sensitive to fluctuations in the international oil market have made them highly vulnerable. In addition, the periodic political tensions emanating from the Iran-Iraq War of 1980-1988 and the Persian Gulf War of 1991 have made OPEC's continued viability highly uncertain.

Inflation and Exploitation

Because OPEC nations are Third World countries, for them the "new order" is not a threat to the world's survival, but a new economic reality—a transfer of wealth from the industrial world to a group of oil producers. They blame inflation and past colonial exploitation as the main reasons for the higher price of oil. To a certain extent, inflation in the Western world may be blamed for the losses in the purchasing power of the petrodollar. But it is not external inflation alone which brings anxiety to OPEC. They, too, face severe domestic inflation, which has become increasingly uncontrollable as more and more money is pumped into the hitherto underdeveloped economies. External inflation is also contributing to decreased savings of petrodollars in foreign bank accounts, but cannot be easily offset by again raising oil prices, since the money saved by this measure comes at the expense of many other nations that are already on the verge of collapse from paying exorbitant petrobills.

It was the Western oil companies that developed the oil resources of the Third World. Had there been no Western technology and money available for the development of petroleum, the exporting nations of today would not have readily known that such resources existed under their soil. Of these nations, only Saudi Arabia has demonstrated a "reasonable" attitude on the twin issues of inflation and exploitation. The oil kingdom seldom, if ever, has blamed the oil companies or, for that matter, the Western nations for inflation and colonial exploitation. Saudi Arabia depends almost wholly on its one-crop economy—oil—for its short- and long-term prosperity. Since it cannot currently spend all of its petrodollars wisely, it is therefore banking on the future, and has invested widely throughout the industrialized world.

Impact on the Third World

The Third World countries, as OPEC saw it, for years had been attempting to lift themselves up by their bootstraps, but the problems they faced in their efforts to develop themselves were, for many of them, overwhelming. The expectation of most of these ex-colonial nations was that, once freed, they could realize their dreams of a more rewarding life quickly. But this has not actually materialized. Instead, corruption, poor planning, one-party governments, tribalism, and the detritus of colonial administrations have left a legacy of economic and political chaos for many of these states.

OPEC is viewed in the Third World as a symbolic leader in the fight to benefit non-Western people in general, and the oil producing countries in particular. Feelings of anger, resentment, protest, and revolt are clearly directed against the West. But as we will see, the effects often boomerang. Higher oil prices, through which the OPEC nations simultaneously try to punish the former colonial powers, and benefit themselves, actually hurts the other Third World countries to a much greater degree than the industrialized West. Ironically, they have become even poorer than before. Yet, despite their enhanced suffering, the Third World countries have stood united with OPEC, deriving no more than psychic satisfaction and the promise of future help. It is common for such nations to blame the former colonial powers for their ills, and they derive a certain emotional satisfaction from their identification with OPEC. The sight of once mighty and affluent nations being humiliated and crippled is a source of happiness amidst otherwise unhappy lives. With the help of OPEC, the Third World hopes to achieve its economic independence—a faint hope, at best, and one which is quite likely self-illusionary.

In fact, the impact of the 1973-74 energy crisis was worldwide: not a single oil-importing state, no matter how large or small, rich or poor, escaped the steep rise in oil prices. As a direct result, Third World development plans were postponed, cut back, or cancelled in every one of these countries, although the economic impact of the price hikes varied widely. Two atypical examples are India and Bangladesh; the former is the largest of the poor nations, and latter is the poorest of the poor. In India, an official estimate showed that higher oil prices could wipe out half of the country's foreign reserves.[10]

The long-term consequences of high oil prices are serious indeed. Third World states long refrained from criticizing OPEC, partly out of fear, and partly from a feeling of solidarity. But when promised economic assistance from OPEC failed to materialize, they finally began to grumble. "We are forced into a corner," said India's petroleum minister.[11] Caught between the two rocks of soaring oil prices and the cost of importing finished goods, the predicament of Bangladesh is such that its president at that time, Ziaur Rahman (Zia), said, "The country's identity as a poor and begging nation in the community of nations [is] humiliating for all."[12] In a desperate attempt to save the near-bankrupt country from complete collapse, President Zia proposed the following measures, among others, while addressing the eleventh special session of the United Nations General Assembly in August 1980: that the OPEC countries effect an immediate fifty-percent reduction in the price of oil for the Least Developed Countries; and that OPEC, with the possible participation of the industrialized world, invest a part of their assets in the LDC.[13]

Further criticism came from a Kenyan journalist in Nairobi: "The Arabs tried to make slaves out of us 500 years ago...and now they're trying to do it again."[14]

The economic situation of virtually every African, Asian, and Latin American country is worse today than it was in 1973. The 1979 *Annual Report* of the International Monetary Fund (IMF) predicted a grim outlook for the world economy because of the worsening oil price situation.[15] To help alleviate the sufferings of the poorer states, the IMF established a ten billion dollar fund for the supplementary financing of nations whose balance-of-payments were in serious difficulty. In the developing countries of Asia, real Gross Domestic Product (GDP) averaged five percent in 1989, the lowest growth rate in more than a decade. In Africa, output growth increased modestly, but the base of this recovery was narrow. In the nations of the Western Hemisphere, output expanded by one and one-half percent in 1989.[16]

As a gesture to lessen the impact of price hikes on the Third World, OPEC announced an allocation of $800 million in aid to these countries, to be disbursed through the OPEC Development Fund, which has a capital of $1.6 billion.[17]

In addition, the secretary-general of the Organization of Arab Petroleum Exporting Countries proposed a twenty-five billion dollar fund to help meet the energy needs of such nations, to be provided by both OPEC and the industrialized world.[18] This underscored the fact that the OPEC and OAPEC nations now wished to be identified with a public posture aimed at improving the distressing situation they had helped to create.

However, the actual priorities of the Arab members of OPEC tend to favor their fellow Arabs and Muslims, plus any non-Arab Third World states who have shown sympathy and support for Arab political objectives. OPEC and OAPEC nations have channeled funds through such lofty-sounding organizations as the OPEC Special Fund, the Arab Bank for Economic Development, the OAPEC Special Fund, the Arab Monetary Fund, the Kuwait Fund for Arab Economic Development, the Saudi Development Fund, and the Abu Dhabi Fund for Economic and Social Development.[19]

Much of the economic assistance given by the Arab members of OPEC to other Muslim states is used to buy arms or to develop showy but superfluous public projects. In a lengthy article on Pakistan's atomic capability, the *Washington Post* reported that Libya, a Muslim member of OPEC, together with several other Islamic oil nations, may have been supporting Pakistan's program of building an "Islamic Bomb."[20] How much money has actually been provided for the project is unknown, because Islamic donations are not recorded.

The Muslim members of OPEC also provide nearly three million skilled, semi-skilled, and unskilled jobs. These migrant workers, who sent home five and one-half billion dollars in earnings between 1975-79,[21] provided a cheap labor pool that greatly benefitted Saudi Arabia and its neighbors.

Despite this economic assistance, more than one billion people in the LDCs face a drastically lower economic situation. One of the principal causes of this calamity is, according to reports prepared by the World Bank, the increase in the price of oil.[22]

Moreover, the effects of the increases on the Third World has been far more devastating than on industrial countries, as the poor nations have relatively little or no room for cutting their oil imports until broader adjustments ensue. Their economic hardships are not considered fundamental to the global economic order.

The escalation in oil prices has also had a dramatic impact on international trade balances and monetary debts, causing higher trade deficits in almost all of the oil-importing countries. While the rich nations have managed, with their greater economic flexibility, to stave off disaster, the poorer countries of the Third World have accumulated massive debt burdens which they will probably never be able to repay.

Even in the 1980s, the annual reports of the World Bank and International Monetary Fund showed the plight of the poorest oil-importing countries steadily growing worse. The depletion of foreign reserves poses difficult problems in financing external deficits. The growing disparity between the oil haves and have-nots has contributed to both international financial chaos and misunderstanding.

Effect on the Industrialized World

The impact of the price increases on the industrialized First World has also been severe:

1) OPEC's continual price hikes are a major contributing cause of worldwide inflation. The real cost of producing a barrel of oil is about twenty-five cents, but OPEC has sold it for as much as thirty-six dollars per barrel, a level which dropped to eighteen dollars by the mid-1980s. This inflated price has no doubt been the single most important cause of inflation in the world since 1973. The market's anticipation of supply disruption, the so-called "war premium," led anxious traders to bid prices up to as high as forty dollars per barrel in October 1990, and prices remained about eight to ten dollars more than what it might have been in the absence of a crisis—about eighteen or twenty dollars per barrel, according to most estimates. For motorists, the war premium added twenty cents or more to the price of a gallon of gasoline, to a total of about $1.16 per gallon.

2) In the early 1980s, economic growth rates in the industrialized nations suffered their greatest decline since the Great Depression of the 1930s. The Western world grew at a rate of just over one percent in 1980, compared with 3.3 percent in 1979. This recession was a major contributor to unemployment in the industrialized countries, and the same thing happened after the 1973 oil price increases.[23] While the West had recovered some economic

ground by 1986, many of the old industries (e.g., steel), have not come back, and, as of 1991, seem permanently affected.

3)   OPEC price hikes have created the unusual economic phenomenon called "stagflation," in which policies to reduce inflation increase unemployment, and policies to reduce unemployment increase inflation. Economists do not know how to handle this vicious cycle. They can control inflation or recession, but not both at the same time. The OPEC nations were also affected directly by the West's economic ills, since their surplus funds were often invested in Western banks.

4)   The standard of living in the entire industrialized world declined and has continued to do so for most people. This makes OPEC and its fellow travelers happy. Some of the comforts and conveniences that were once the hallmarks of the industrialized nations have vanished—but not all, and not for all classes. Adjustments in heating and air conditioning settings, reduced speed limits, smaller cars, and curtailed pleasure trips and vacations have become common in the United States, Western Europe, and Japan.

5)   Societal divisions in the West began to widen along economic lines, a phenomenon not seen there in generations, and a direct reversal of previous long-term trends. As a result, the entire capitalistic and democratic system which depends on it have become vulnerable, and potentially subject to internal strife or political polarization as the gap between the haves and have-nots in society continues to grow.

        OPEC was able to accomplish the above by taking advantage of a critical situation during the Arab-Israeli war of 1973. When the Arab countries began their embargo, OPEC sought to exploit the situation further by unilaterally increasing prices. Thereafter, OPEC successfully increased the price of oil whenever it wished until the oil glut of the mid-1980s. Although OPEC is not a monolithic organization and the divergencies among its members are well known, it can boast of the following accomplishments:

1)   OPEC was able to check unilateral price reductions by the oil companies.

2)   It achieved increased prices, higher tax rates, and compensation for inflation.

3)   Royalties have been eliminated as credits against tax liabilities.

4)   Marketing allowances have been reduced as deductions from production costs.

5)   OPEC coordinates member countries' legislation regarding oil, and it trains experts and technicians who could replace at any time the multinational oil

companies working under special contract in many OPEC countries.

6) Full ownership of each nation's own oil reserves has been realized by all OPEC members.

7) Until the period of 1983-86, prices were determined unilaterally by OPEC (this changed, however, in 1983-84).

8) From a relatively powerless entity, OPEC has become a major global force, although not a dominant one.

Events since 1973 and particularly since the 1979 Iranian Revolution (and Iran's subsequent war with Iraq) continue to make apparent the inherent danger of a world that depends on an insecure supply of petroleum energy, without which neither the pre-industrialized Third World nor the industrialized First World can survive. "The year 1979 was one of grievous setbacks for the future of the oil supply of the Western world, its economic and financial prospects, its strategic capabilities, and its political stability."[24]

In response to the Arab oil embargo and the Iranian Revolution, the industrialized world has built up their own substantial oil reserves. As a result of additional supplies, plus conservation measures, coupled with the Saudi decision to increase production in order to compensate for the loss of Iranian oil in the world market, the consuming nations have managed to avoid any serious energy crisis. Still, OPEC decided to raise prices again in December 1980, increasing it to thirty-six dollars per barrel on January 1, 1981.[25]

The crucial role that Saudi Arabia played by increasing production from eight and one-half million to over ten million barrels a day represented a determined effort to maintain friendship with Western consumers, particularly American ones. It also allowed Saudi Arabia to flex its muscles before the other OPEC nations, especially its enemies Iran and Libya, to force them toward a more moderate policy, and to let the Saudis dictate all future oil matters.

A breakthrough for OPEC—and particularly for Saudi Arabia, which had been exporting considerably more oil than it needed for its own revenues—came at a March 1982 meeting in Vienna, when OPEC agreed for the first time to put a ceiling on oil production. It also agreed not to lower the thirty-four-dollar market price, which already was being sold at lower prices elsewhere on the spot market. Indeed, OPEC is now what Saudi Arabia makes of it. Saudi Arabia is able to manipulate the production, prices, and policies of OPEC to its own advantage and to the benefit of its friends.

Saudi Arabia is concerned with the damage that has been inflicted on the most severely affected nations of Asia and Africa, and believes that excessively high oil prices encourage not only the conservation of oil in the industrialized world, but also increase wildcat production of non-OPEC oil and oil substitutes.

OPEC's interests are not those of the consumer; no amount of wishful thinking will make them so. As mentioned earlier, the transfer of power from the oil companies and consumers to OPEC has already taken place. OPEC will always try to prove that it is in control by keeping prices at the highest level possible. Its failure to do so since 1983 was a humiliating admission of defeat, as uncontrollable market forces resulted in a sudden collapse of oil price levels in 1986.

The great war over the world's vital resources has just begun, with many more battles and skirmishes yet to be fought. It is already apparent that the real losses in this struggle will be neither OPEC nor the West, but those Third World states who have no oil resources of their own. For the interim, the West would be foolhardy to assume that the present oil glut will continue indefinitely. As certain as death and taxes are, prices, driven by forces over which OPEC has only minimal control, will soon increase once again to staggering levels. If the West fails to plan now for alternative sources of energy to offset future oil shortages, it is no better than the lemmings that fall to their death—and will surely meet the same fate in the end.

VI.

THE MYTH AND REALITY
OF CHINESE OIL

Until recently, the People's Republic of China (P.R.C.) was a tightly closed country, a sleeping giant not ready to be awakened. However, its more recent leaders have mobilized the most populous nation in the world, with its vast multitude of ill-fed, ill-housed, and ill-clad Chinese through the "four modernizations." Increased emphasis has been placed on the development of agriculture, industry, national defense, and science and technology, and has led to a gradual opening of the country to outside influences, and even to small capitalistic ventures. As a result of freer travel in and out of China, and an increase in the dissemination of information about the country from post-Maoist leaders, outsiders are now able to obtain a more balanced and perhaps more sobering picture of contemporary Chinese society.

China has vast natural resources and a substantial industrial base. However, except for the first decade following the establishment of the People's Republic, no detailed industrial and economic figures have been published. Although the Chinese economy is already the world's sixth largest,[1] we must accept the fact that China is the first world power to veil almost all of its industrial and economic development in secrecy. Because the Chinese do not publish detailed statistics, a reasonably accurate assessment of Chinese oil capacity, not to mention production, is difficult to ascertain. Despite the speculative character of any study on China, it seems worthwhile to evaluate whatever information is available on Chinese oil because of its growing international importance.

China is the world's oldest oil-producing country, a natural gas field having been discovered as early as the second century B.C. The extraction of oil in China through percussion drilling with cables dates back to the first century B.C.[2] This field, located in Sichuan province, is still in operation today. Nevertheless, oil development in its modern sense did not take place in China before the establishment of the People's Republic in 1949. The highest annual output of oil before 1950 was about 300,000 tons, including shale oil. The newly founded regime launched a vigorous drive in search of oil and gave priority to the survey and development of new sources of petroleum.

China's efforts to build an oil industry were bolstered by the technical assistance it received from the Soviet Union, beginning with its first Five-Year Plan in 1953-57. During this period, the Soviets made vital contributions to the development of China's oil industry. Their total investment there during this period is reported to have been about $800 million. Geological areas surveyed in these years covered about 290,000 square kilometers, and exploration wells were dug throughout this area. This effort involved Soviet geologists as well as oil drilling engineers and technicians, and it was from these technical experts that the Chinese learned the basics of the oil industry. Without such groundwork, the development of China's oil fields and production capacity would have been much delayed. Other Soviet bloc countries providing assistance were Czechoslovakia, Hungary, Poland, East Germany, and Romania.

One of the most notable events in the history of Chinese oil development was the discovery of the Daqing oil field in Northeast China in 1959, followed quickly by other major finds. Production from these fields enabled China in 1963 to achieve basic self-sufficiency in oil. The annual oil yield seven years later was increased to eighteen million tons, approximately equivalent to fourteen days' production in the American oil industry. In terms of its oil output in 1970, China ranked with Mexico and Oman.

China's oil production, barely 120,000 tons annually upon the founding of the People's Republic, exceeded seventy million tons in 1974, and China's recent output may have reached as high as 400 million tons annually[3], a figure comparable to the output of such giant producers as Saudi Arabia, the United States, and the Soviet Union. However, other experts estimate China's output at 130 million tons, an amount which seems more plausible. Even if we accept the lower estimate, China's oil production is roughly comparable with that of Iran, Kuwait, Venezuela, Nigeria, Libya, and Canada.

Close observers of the Chinese economy have long known that Chinese estimates must be regarded with some skepticism. This unfortunate situation seems to be the reason behind such discrepancies in figures relating to China's industrial output. Some of the most fanciful estimates have emanated from Western sources. According to some projections, Chinese oil production was to have reached as high as 500 million tons by the late 1980s. This seems on the surface highly unlikely. A more conservative estimate was that China's annual oil production might have reached the 200-million-ton mark by 1987.

To forecast China's production in the future, we must consider several factors. China's geological factors make her one of the world's greatest potential oil producers, perhaps the last major untapped reserve. But the rapid development of new oil fields has been curbed by several factors, including the inability of China's storage, refining, distributing, and exporting facilities to keep up with production. Self-reliance, one of the dominant principles of China's economic development, is apt to slow down all production, including petroleum, and this is a serious drawback.

Thirteen countries besides China produce more than two and one-half billion tons of oil annually.[4] A comparison with the Soviet Union may be useful, as it is the only country in the modern age that has been able to expand oil production from fifty million tons to over 400 million tons annually. The Soviet Union started its expansion from a fifty-million-ton base in 1945-55. At that time, the Soviets' output of oil drilling and refining equipment was quite inadequate, although they did have the advantage of a strong industrial base. But to finance the exploration of her rich oil resources, and to obtain the advanced drilling, transportation, and refinery technology that was needed, the Soviet Union entered into long-term bilateral agreements with Western European countries and Japan. Conversely, China has always opposed long-term arrangements for the development of its oil resources. The oil development process will take longer and will be less efficient, but, considering China's tenacity, the P.R.C. could make satisfactory progress independently, if it obtains sufficient foreign assistance in an indirect manner.

China's Oil Targets

In spite of the uncertainties, discrepancies, and misinformation, Beijing had, to quote Selig S. Harrison, a noted authority on Chinese oil and Asian politics, a "better than fifty-fifty chance" of reaching its annual goal of 400 million tons by 1990.[5] Yet production failed to reach this goal, and although Chinese oil production is expected to increase, domestic consumption will also rise as the P.R.C. starts to industrialize and to improve the living standards of its people. The exportable balance, if any, will most likely go to Japan and Southeast Asian countries, where political and economic benefits can be maximized.

Increasing exports of oil may well result in production boosts. China's active effort since 1973—the year of the Arab oil embargo—to find foreign customers for her oil reveal that the Chinese intend to use any future price hikes to earn much-needed foreign exchange credits. China made her debut among oil-exporting countries at a time when the industrialized nations were troubled by an unprecedented energy crisis, and when many countries, including Japan, foresaw a gloomy economic future for the world in general.

Chinese oil exports have attracted worldwide attention since the first shipments were made to Japan in 1973, and many exaggerated predictions of their future magnitude were publicized by uncritical observers. Although exports to Japan increased from one million tons initially to 8.2 million tons in 1975, thoughtful critics concluded that China's future as an oil-exporter was limited. Japan tried again in 1976 to negotiate at least a five-year agreement for oil imports from China, but was unsuccessful. On February 16, 1978, China and Japan signed an eight-year agreement under which bilateral trade, including oil, would grow to about twenty billion dollars over the ensuing three to four years. The agreement projected that Chinese exports of oil to Japan would increase to fifteen million tons by 1982. Following former trade and industry minister Toshio Komoto's visit to Beijing in September 1978, it was reported that Japan might import as much as forty to fifty million tons of Chinese oil per year by 1985. It soon became apparent that such a projection was unrealistic. In order to increase imports of Chinese oil to that level, a significant change in Japanese refining facilities would be required, because Chinese oil is high in wax and nitrogen compounds. It would probably cost Japan ten billion dollars to improve its equipment to the point where it could handle such capacity.[6]

China's oil reserves are of paramount political significance to the region.

As soon as the P.R.C. signed its oil deal with Japan, it broke-off negotiations with the Soviet Union for construction of a pipeline to the Yellow Sea, which was to secure large-scale oil supplies to Japan.

In November 1973, China offered to sell Hong Kong diesel oil, and made its first attempt to supply oil to the Philippines. At the same time, China showed a willingness to deal with Australia, and began deliveries of oil to Thailand. The decision to export petroleum to Thailand again suggests the political character of the P.R.C.'s trading policies, since it made the gesture of goodwill to one of the last countries in Asia that had not yet entered into diplomatic relations with Beijing.

Difficulties in forecasting China's role as an oil exporter are, as already mentioned, due to a lack of officially published figures for oil production from which to extrapolate, and our ignorance of the P.R.C.'s long-term intentions, including the possible deliberate restraint of its economic development for political reasons. From its modernization program and other forms of development, it does appear that the regime in China is willing to use its oil to develop the country. Thus far, however, it has only been offering for export surplus petroleum which it has been unable to use at home, due both to a lack of industry and a shortage of storing and refining capacity. This may well change as China's domestic consumption increases.

By 1979 China was producing two million barrels per day of oil. A decade later, China had improved on that performance by nearly forty percent, with an estimated 2.78 million barrels produced daily in 1989. Continuing this record of progress is becoming increasingly difficult, however. While China's total petroleum resources are estimated to be huge—more than 300 sedimentary basins onshore covering four and one-half million square kilometers and 170 potentially oil-bearing onshore structures have been identified by geological surveys—planners have been excessively optimistic about the extent of China's reserves to be discovered in the near future. Oft-quoted official figures for total oil resources are 469 billion barrels of oil (a comparable figure for Saudi Arabia is 315 billion barrels.)[7]

The following table lists China's oil production history and forecast through the year 2000:

TABLE 8
Petroleum Production History and Forecast: 1987-2000
(millions of barrels/day)

Actual		Estimated			Projected
1987	1988	1989	1990	1995	2000
2.69	2.74	2.78	2.94	3.50* 3.30**	4.00* 3.75**

*CNPC estimate; **Estimate by Wu Kang, East-West Center
Source: *The China Business Review* (March-April 1990).

A basic policy decision which the People's Republic must make is whether its oil sector should merely keep step with domestic requirements, or should attempt to produce a surplus that could be used to finance a modernization of all segments of its economy. The Chinese leaders have long displayed an ambivalent attitude toward the benefits of economic specialization as opposed to self-reliance. Still, China is now actively importing Western technology and industrial plants to the point where it has substantially increased its trade deficit. Hence, there is a good possibility that China will try to expand its oil exports to meet this debt.

It should be noted that there are absolutely no Chinese-generated figures for its mineral reserves, including oil. However, outside sources have stated that Chinese reserves are enormous. Estimates of onshore reserves range from 2.7 to seventy billion tons.[8] The *Christian Science Monitor*, on September 15, 1973, cited a figure of between eight and ten billion tons. More recent estimates have been revised substantially upward, ranging from ten billion to fifty billion tons.[9]

These figures should suffice to show the speculative character of such estimates in the absence of official data. Selig S. Harrison believes that "depending on the outcome of the offshore boundary scramble, the addition of an offshore dimension could at least double the Chinese oil potential, even by relatively conservative estimates."[10]

In assessing China's offshore progress in oil and exploration, it is necessary to bear in mind the new sensitivity of long-outstanding disputes over China's sea boundaries. A growing Chinese offshore capability could foreshadow significant clashes of interests with Taiwan, South Korea, Vietnam, Japan, the Philippines, and the Soviet Union.

Offshore Oil Rights

The major uncertainty in determining Southeast Asian oil rights is the questionable status of conflicting offshore border claims in the East China Sea, the Yellow Sea, the Taiwan Strait, and the South China Sea. This has continued to complicate relations between China and its eight neighbors who also have made counterclaims of varying magnitude to these regions and their underlying resources.[11]

China's ability to develop oil surpluses for export depends to a great degree on whether major oil deposits do in fact exist beneath the waters of the East China and Yellow Seas, and on how the conflicting claims to those areas are ultimately resolved. The positions of the various claimants are as follows:

1) Japan follows the "median line" doctrine and claims roughly the eastern half of the East China Sea.

2) South Korea uses the median line doctrine in the Yellow Sea, but in the East China Sea applies the doctrine of "natural extension" of its shoreline out to a depth of 200 meters.

3) Taiwan, making its claim on behalf of "China," argues that the area in question is China's continental shelf, and claims all of the Yellow Sea and the East China Sea up to the Okinawa Trench.

4) China, on the other hand, has told Japan that she would like to explore jointly the oil reserves in and around the Senkaku Islands, near Okinawa in the East China Sea, and to seek American participation in the proposed venture.[12]

   The United States administered the Senkaku Islands from 1945 until it returned them to Japan in 1972. At the time, it was widely believed that Japan needed to exercise its claims to the Senkakus in order to secure rights to part of the continental shelf. Taipei still argues that Japan cannot take over the Okinawa Trench, but Tokyo, citing the precedent of Norway's claim in the North Sea, now asserts the median line doctrine, using the Ryukyus as a baseline.

5) China's offshore claims stretch all the way to Vietnam, Malaysia, Indonesia, and the Philippines.[13]

6) China objects to the claims and offshore activities by these parties, but has never clearly enunciated its own position.

7) North Korea's position is not known, but its claims may overlap with those of China.

The status of the various disputes created by the above conflicting claims differs widely:

1) The claims of Beijing and Taipei are in total conflict, but this difference is slowly being submerged in the more fundamental disagreement over which claimant is the sole legal government in China. As Taiwan becomes a non-state, its claim to China's continental shelf is largely academic. An important fact is that Taipei has not granted oil concessions in the Yellow Sea or the Western half of the East China Sea.

2) Tokyo and Taipei have in the past granted conflicting oil concessions, but neither seems to be selling actual drilling sites in the contested areas. The People's Republic and Japan seem most interested now in promoting some kind of a joint venture.

3) Taipei and Seoul have avoided pushing their overlapping claims.

4) The People's Republic has denounced Seoul for unilaterally bringing foreign

oil exploration companies into Chinese coastal areas.

5) Tokyo and Seoul concluded an agreement in 1974 for joint exploration of the disputed areas, but Beijing denounced this agreement as an "infringement of China's sovereignty."

6) Hanoi, Kuala Lumpur, Jakarta, and Manila have remained silent concerning any offshore claims, possibly because they want to avoid a conflict with Beijing.

Offshore Oil Dilemma

If China does adopt a policy of greatly expanding its offshore oil exploration, which seems likely, it cannot postpone dealing with the problem of conflicting claims to the seabed off its coast. The Chinese leaders may face a dilemma. If they accept a median line settlement, which could easily be negotiated with the Japanese and South Koreans, they may have to give up a large area claimed by the Taiwanese.

Selig S. Harrison poses a scenario in which a possible conciliatory posture by Taiwan toward China might result in the phasing out of most of the Taiwanese offshore concessions. He believes that under this scenario China might treat Taiwan as an autonomous province:

> This change on the part of Taipei is paralleled by the successful conclusion of a Sino-Japanese friendship treaty and an increasing Japanese "tilt" toward Beijing in the Tokyo-Beijing-Moscow Triangle. Japan and China then reach a median line agreement in which a greatly weakened Taiwan is tacitly treated as a province of China and is induced (by economic rewards from Washington, Tokyo, and Beijing) to acquiesce in the new dispensation by quietly phasing out most of its offshore concessions to the north of the island.[14]

It can be assumed that, in the long term, oil supplies will continue to be limited while world demand will increase and that much of the world will still rely on imported petroleum to meet the bulk of its energy needs. Under such circumstances, it appears that any substantial oil exports would give China important leverage. China sees in Japan an example of the impact of oil shortages and counts on it both as a supplier of industrial hardware and technology and as a local buyer of Chinese oil.

Because of the low cost of transporting Chinese oil to Japan, China would presumably charge premium prices, in much the same way as Libya does from its European importers. Japan, anxious to diversify its oil supply sources, would welcome the emergence of the P.R.C. as a new supplier. Such a development would be a boon to Japan, which is seeking an outlet for its industrial products to cope with the rising tide of protectionism in Western Europe and the United States. The improvement in Sino-Japanese relations has also helped in the creation of a *rapprochement* in Sino-American relations, including the establishment of diplomatic ties between Beijing and Washington.

Sino-Japanese relations became strained when the two nations failed in 1975 to agree on the thorny antihegemony clause in connection with the conclusion of a Sino-Japanese peace treaty. Both nations were also stalemated over their positions on off-shore oil rights in the East China Sea. Tokyo was further subjected to mounting pressure from Moscow not to sign the treaty. However, the Chinese felt there was much to be learned from the industrial experience of Japan, which was the first Asian country to modernize successfully. China had other reasons to be flexible in its approach to Japan. Chinese foreign policy was geared to the containment of Soviet hegemony by forming a broad united front with as many countries as possible against the USSR, including the United States, Japan, and Western Europe. The signing of a peace treaty with Japan containing an antihegemony clause would constitute a major foreign policy victory. The Chinese also indicated their readiness to take whatever steps might be necessary to scrap the Sino-Soviet alliance, which contained a clause offensive to the Japanese. Thus, on August 23, 1978, the Japan-China Treaty of Peace and Friendship was signed by Beijing.

In the wake of the peace treaty, Sino-Japanese relations have perceptively improved. Oil is the only Chinese export of any great interest to the Japanese, and the peace treaty projected that Japanese imports of Chinese oil would increase from seven million tons in 1978 to fifteen million by 1982. To be sure, there are potential sources of friction between China and Japan, such as disputed claims over several offshore islands that may possess rich oil deposits. But as long as the Chinese and American conflict with the Soviet Union persists, and as long as China needs hardware and technology from Japan, these issues are likely to remain dormant.

Since the Shanghai Communiqué of 1972, the United States has looked to China as a potential source of petroleum, and as a market for American technology, military hardware, and consumer goods. American policy has shifted from direct encouragement of U.S. concessionary links with Japan, Taiwan, and South Korea to a more flexible approach attuned to the new American relationship with the P.R.C. The U.S. government has displayed some nervousness over oil exploration rights granted by Taipei to American oil companies in disputed offshore areas, and has warned them not to explore for oil in these areas.

Since diplomatic relations were established between the People's Republic and the United States in 1979, China has shown a willingness to adopt a policy of expanding its oil exports through the help of Western, including American, technological and financial assistance.

Although the United States might not actually receive any of China's petroleum in the near future, it would benefit along with the other oil importing countries if the emergence of China as a major exporter contributed to a general loosening of oil supplies in the world, including a drop in prices. Also, if American oil companies became involved in large-scale oil exploration off the China coast, a mutually beneficial trade relationship might well develop.

The United States is now exporting various important goods to China, including grain (especially corn, soybeans, and wheat), cotton, polyester fibers, oil drilling equipment, trucks, and automobile parts. The U.S. Commerce Department predicted in 1980 that Sino-American trade would soon reach the ten billion dollar mark.[15] China is resorting to "compensation trade" in an effort to convince foreign companies to accept Chinese products as payment, thereby reducing actual exchanges of cash.

In 1990, the total volume of U.S.-Sino trade amounted to $11.77 billion, including $5.18 billion worth of exports to the United States and $6.59 billion worth of imports from the United States, with a deficit of $1.41 billion on the Chinese side. The portion from the U.S. in China's total imports has been expanding continuously, which shows that American goods are enhancing their position in the Chinese market.[16]

China must import grain in order to feed its huge population, and the United States has more exportable food grains than any other nation on earth. The Chinese have been making a major oil expansion effort which, according to *Fortune Magazine*, could result in an annual growth rate of ten percent.[17] A new and symbolic diversification of American oil import sources would represent an effort to reduce its dependence on OPEC, and to acquire more leverage to control oil prices. If China could so quickly increase its petroleum shipments to Japan following the Arab oil embargo of 1973, it can probably increase its oil production further and sell the surplus to the United States. Much depends on the hidden political agenda of the current Chinese government.

Reagan-Bush Policy

Although President Reagan was known to be a conservative supporter of Taiwan, he adopted, as official U.S. policy, a more pragmatic view of the situation, and thus sought an accommodation with mainland China. China itself has been moving in the same direction, and is now closer to the West than at any time since the days of Chiang Kai-shek.

In May 1991, President Bush asked Congress to extend most-favored-nation trade benefits to China for an additional year, calling it the best chance of influencing Chinese policy. He also moved to retaliate against China for providing long-range missiles to Pakistan by clamping down on sales of high-tech equipment and computers. In addition to American technology, China needs capital and markets. On the other hand, the U.S. needs China's market and reasonably priced commodities. Therefore, it is mutually beneficial to enhance cooperation between the two nations.

Increased cooperation between the P.R.C. and the United States would not only lead to a relaxation of tensions, but would also sow the seeds of an emerging capitalist-communist "condominium." Considering these possibilities requires that China be ideologically less doctrinaire and more politically stable, and that the Bush administration continue to adopt an increasingly more realistic and pragmatic approach reminiscent of the Republican presidencies of Richard Nixon and Gerald Ford.

As a participant in the world oil market but not a member of OPEC (the members of which are all non-communist states), China is likely to take an independent stand on issues affecting its interests and the interests of its allies. It may verbally support OPEC's policy of maintaining high prices in order to weaken capitalist economies and to reduce the economic power of the capitalist world. However, in the event of a future Arab oil embargo or an embargo by other nations against the West and Japan, China might well supply them with oil, in much the same way as Iran did during the 1973-74 Arab-Israeli war.

On the other hand, China may offer moral and political support for positions taken by individual producing countries, or even sometimes by OPEC. This stance meshes well with China's self-generated image as the champion of the Third World, which includes all OPEC members, in opposition to the interests of the United States and the other industrialized oil-importing countries.

Continuing increases in oil prices are politically, as well as economically, advantageous to China. As a potential energy exporter to the West, it is more than likely that the P.R.C. will continue to demand high prices for its own oil exports. In that case, China will support OPEC demands for higher prices, and will back the efforts of other producing countries to raise their share of the petrodollars at the expense of the oil have-nots.

An important facet of China's oil posture is its continuing political conflict with the Soviet Union. Some observers speculate that China's sale of oil to Japan was an attempt to sabotage Soviet-Japanese cooperation in Siberian energy development. It is also believed that to increase its oil potential further, China has been renewing its claims on Russian-held territories in Siberia and Central Asia.

Japan appears likely to attach greater importance to its oil links with China than with the Soviet Union, which continues to occupy Japanese-claimed territory. China looms large in Japanese trade calculations. Japanese markets in Asia, while expanding, have not compensated for the declining growth in Japanese exports to Western countries, and the P.R.C., with one billion people and a fast-developing economy, is viewed as a more promising trade frontier than is the Soviet Union. This is another bone of contention in Sino-Soviet relations.

Thus far, the joint interests of the Soviet Union, the United States, and Japan in mining energy resources in the Soviet Union have had little impact on the Chinese oil industry, or on China's access to the world oil market. But this could change, particularly during the next ten years or so, with continuing heavy Western and Japanese dependence on foreign oil.

At present, the Communist giants play a relatively minuscule role in the world's oil trade. The Soviet Union supplies oil mostly to its satellite countries and to some Western European nations. China provides oil primarily to non-communist Third World countries and Japan. Most experts agree that the Chinese oil industry is continuing to develop while Soviet oil production has probably reached its peak, or has even declined somewhat. However, there still remains uncertainties about

China's oil potential.

Although China possesses vast energy resources, the economy has chronically suffered from inadequate energy supplies. About twenty percent of the P.R.C.'s industrial capacity lies idle each year because of insufficient energy, while in the countryside more than 300 million peasants still do not have even a single light bulb in their homes.

The lure of oil took Amoco's subsidiary company, Amoco Orient Petroleum, to China in 1991 to produce oil at an annual rate of at least 60,000 barrels per day. This is the largest foreign offshore oil development contract in the P.R.C., and the venture is likely to pave the way for new downstream projects, including a petrochemical complex and refinery.

Oil development programs for the 1990s place top priority on maintaining China's oil output. In the 1980s, problems became more acute, as rising demand put pressure on the Chinese government to increase investment. Foreign analysts forecast an annual five percent in China's domestic oil consumption throughout the 1990s. Current growth in oil production has been running only two-to-four percent, however, and could reach zero growth in the 1995-2005 period without heavy investment. That investment is more readily available from foreign companies than from China. But, if current policies are continued, foreign participation will be largely confined to offshore involvement. In that case, the P.R.C.'s oil production may not increase significantly. As a consequence, exports are likely to be reduced, and domestic demand will be constrained as well. This situation may force China to become even a net importer of oil by the late 1990s or early 2000s.

VII.

SOVIET OIL STRATEGY IN THE WORLD

The beginning of the oil price war of 1973-74 and the confrontation between OPEC and the West altered the Soviet perception of its future relations with the Arab and other OPEC states. This fundamental alteration in Soviet oil politics has opened up new opportunities for the Soviets to solidify their relations with the oil-producing states.

The century of Western influence and domination in the Middle East has made OPEC naturally hostile toward the West. In contrast, their attitude toward the Soviets, not colored by any previous record of colonial-based relations, has been emotionally neutral, except on the question of Muslim rights in the USSR. This being so, in any struggle for power and influence in the Third World, where the Soviet Union and the West have much the same political and economic means, the USSR often has had a certain initial psychological advantage.

However, there is no one-to-one relationship between economic penetration and political adventure in a world in which both the West and the Soviet Union serve as alternate suppliers. Attempts to exploit economic dependency for political leverage are bound to cause the threatened nation to appeal for help to the rival supplier.

In this atmosphere, OPEC nations consider themselves most secure when both the West and the Soviet Union continue to compete for their favor. They are also confident that if their independence is threatened by one side, the other side will offer assistance.

By now, it is clearer than ever that OPEC is as dependent on Western oil revenues for the economic progress that is essential to their political stability as the industrialized nations are dependent upon OPEC for fuel. The more the subsistence economy of OPEC is transformed by national development programs, the larger the constituency touched by a loss of oil revenues.

The extension of Soviet influence in OPEC has been erratic, and has often failed to provide clear guidelines for assessing overall Soviet strategy. Yet, the Soviet Union is a preeminent power in global oil politics because it is sometimes the world's largest single producer of oil, and because it is in the forefront of other energy developments. The Soviet Union, according to a CIA study, sells more oil to the West than to its allies in the Communist bloc.[1]

Many commentators view the Soviet energy situation enigmatically. But we will try here to avoid the narrowmindedness which often surrounds the subject, and deal with the issues evenhandedly. Four topics merit special attention: (1) Soviet oil prospects; (2) Soviet friendship with their comrades in Eastern Europe; (3) Soviet relations with the First World; and (4) Soviet strategy in the oil-rich Middle East.

The political and economic aspects of Soviet oil policy are inseparable, both internally and externally. The Soviet Union is a major exporter, as well as importer, of oil. It has repeatedly resorted to using oil as a political weapon against such neighbors as the People's Republic of China, Yugoslavia, Romania, and Finland. The Soviets have also sought to limit Western power by encouraging the nationalization of the multinational oil companies. With the hope of partially crippling the capitalist world's economy, it further supported the 1973-74 Arab oil embargo. To contain China, the Soviets have invited Western and Japanese oil companies to participate in oil exploration, drilling, and development in Siberia.

The Bolshevik government in the Soviet Union inherited well-developed oil fields from the tsar, the fields in Baku and Caucasus having been developed with West European financing. As a result, the Soviets had become the world's leading oil producer prior to World War I. The initial years of the new Soviet regime were devoted to the reconstruction and further development of its petroleum resources, a move which was temporarily halted because of Soviet involvment in international disputes over the nationalization of oil companies.[2]

Although the Soviets fell to second place among oil exporters, petroleum was still available in abundance. The Soviets used profits from such sales to finance the First Five-Year Plan (1928-32). The USSR supplied 14.3 percent of the oil imported by the Western states during 1930-33.[3] From 1933, however, Soviet oil exports declined, and by the end of the 1930s the USSR was importing oil in anticipation of World War II.[4]

When Germany launched a surprise attack against the Soviet Union in the summer of 1941, eighty percent of Soviet oil production was concentrated in the Caucasus, which was thus a prime target of German bombing. As the war progressed and the USSR faced a grim prospect for survival, Soviet oil production was severly disrupted and output fell drastically. The United States came to the rescue of the Soviets and supplied whatever oil was needed, equivalent to one-fourth of the total Soviet supply. America also increased the USSR's refining capability under the Lend-Lease program,[5] and the Soviets imported additional oil from neighboring Iran. They would remain a net importer of oil until 1954.

Rebuilding the Soviet oil industry proved to be difficult and time-consuming. The expansion of production that finally occurred in the Caucasus was due to great advances in technology, which made possible deep drilling and offshore production. As the Soviets look to the future, they can expect the greatest growth in domestic production to come from Siberia and the Mangyshlak Peninsula in the Caspian Sea. Participation by American and Japanese oil companies in the development of this oil makes sense on economic grounds. An increased output of oil from the Soviet Union will improve the world's oil supply situation and ease mounting pressures on prices. This is one way of diversifying the First World's dependence on a single, highly unreliable source such as OPEC. It may also eventually lead to a Soviet-fuel-for-American-food barter deal. Much depends on the long-term Soviet oil reserves, and on the two superpowers' willingness to cooperate. A Soviet-American unholy alliance, if it materializes, would nip OPEC's oil imperialism in the bud. For mutual benefit, the two superpowers may come to terms to score gains in the new game of oil politics, as evidenced to some degree by their cooperation during the 1991 Persian Gulf War.

Comradeship

For reasons of national security, ideological and economic considerations, and international *realpolitik*, the Soviet Union has important long-term political and economic goals in their Eastern European satellites. Together, they provide a very large captive market for Soviet goods, including petroleum. With a population of more than 100 million people, and an industrial output nearly two-thirds that of the Soviet Union, Eastern Europe serves the USSR as both a bridge and an escape valve to the West. At one time, Eastern Europe was a net exporter of energy, but this surplus has now dwindled, making the area energy deficient, with a consumption rate that is growing faster than Western Europe's. To maintain this vast captive market:

> The Soviet Union has used its control over the oil industry of most communist-ruled states to keep them within the Soviet sphere of influence, and in those situations where states have tried to break away from Soviet hegemony the oil weapon has been applied as a pressure tactic in order to retard such fissiparous tendencies.[6]

Eastern Europe has relatively few oil resources, the only countries with significant production capacity being little Albania, a maverick in Marxist circles, and Romania, once solidly within the Soviet fold. Despite the slow growth of oil production in Eastern Europe, consumption there has increased, the difference being provided by imports from the Soviet Union. The mechanism used by the USSR to manage their economic empire is the Council of Mutual Economic Assistance, commonly known as COMECON or CMEA.

A typical example of Soviet oil policy in Eastern Europe is the case of Romania. At the end of World War II, the USSR occupied Romania and seized much of the American and British oil equipment there, moving it to the Soviet Union. Romania, a vanquished nation, had to pay war reparations to the Soviet Union, including a supply of 1.7 million tons of oil per year for six years.[7] Later, the Soviets extended the term to eight years and ultimately announced that the Romanians would only have to pay half of their reparations. But some British and American researchers maintain that the Soviets actually received more oil than cited in the reparation agreement, the difference being stolen or confiscated.[8] During this period, the Soviets and Romanians established a joint stock company (Sovrompetrol) specifically to manage Soviet-backed oil production in Romania. This so-called "joint company" was in fact a Soviet scheme for legally acquiring about sixty percent of total Romanian oil production.

Other than Romania, few Eastern European countries possess significant petroleum reserves. Poland and Hungary produce some oil, but are far from self-sufficient. Czechoslovakia and Bulgaria have little or no oil. Yugoslavia produces sizable amounts of crude, but still far less than necessary to meet its own growing needs.

Energy consumption rates are increasing rapidly in Eastern Europe. The Soviet Union exports more than half of its oil to Eastern Europe. Recently, the Soviet Union, being unable to meet the growing demands for oil in the COMECON states, has allowed them to import oil from the world market. By allowing its satellites to import OPEC oil, the Soviets hope to sell as much of its production as possible to Western Europe and thereby earn badly needed hard currency. Since 1965, several Eastern European countries have concluded trade pacts with Arab countries and Iran.[9] These agreements have often consisted of exchanging Middle Eastern oil for Eastern European arms and manufactured goods. However, the Europeans are now facing a problem since the newly acquired bargaining power of OPEC nations has made them less interested in bartering oil for goods. This places COMECON and the Soviet Union, as they are chronically short of hard currency, in a very difficult situation. If the lack of hard currency did not pose such a problem, the Eastern European countries could step forward toward economic independence from Moscow by diversifying their sources of oil purchases and other goods.

Other than Eastern Europe, the Soviet Union had, at one time, a large oil market in mainland China. Despite the logistical difficulties in shipping crude halfway around the world from the Black Sea, the Soviets were exporting to China two and one-half to three million tons of petroleum annually in the late 1950s and early 1960s. Soviet advisors, technicians, and oil equipment helped the Chinese develop their oil exploration and drilling capabilities. However, the resulting poltical differences between the two Communist giants led to a reduction in Sino-Soviet trade, and all Soviet oil assistance was terminated.

The First World

The Soviet Union, because it is a significant exporter of oil, gas, and coal and because it also imports oil, has strong political and economic interests throughout the world, including the capitalist countries.

Subsequently, Western press reports stressing the Soviets' supposed need for Western capital and technology to develop their oil resources seem somewhat exaggerated:

> Looking at the Soviet side, there has been considerable talk in the Western press of how the Russians "need" Western capital in order to develop their fuel riches, and of how the construction lags and capital shortages of the Soviet planned economy have led to

problems only the financial and engineering resources of the capitalist world can resolve.[10]

Edward W. Erickson and Leonard Waverman further state that the Soviet Union is fully capable of expanding its fuel output for domestic as well as foreign use. If the price is right—and the the USSR has steadily encouraged OPEC to make the price right—the Soviets are fully capable of increasing their oil production to whatever level they deem proper.[11]

The Siberian dilemma is often cited as an example of Soviet dependence on capitalist technology for oil development. The prospect of developing their Siberian oil fields presented the Soviets with an opportunity to use economics as an instrument of foreign policy. With an eye to containing China, the Soviets invited both Japan and the United States to participate in the development of Siberian petroleum resources. Irrespective of the economic and technical advantages for the USSR, such participation would discourage the West from joining China in an alliance against the Soviet Union, and it would give these nations a stake in preventing any potential Chinese expansion into Siberia, which the Chinese have long claimed as theirs.

Ever since the creation of the Soviet Union in October 1917, the United States has consistently embargoed the export of key technological commodities to the chief Communist state. The U.S. has also pressured its Western allies to restrict their imports of Soviet oil. In addition, the multinational oil companies, under instructions from their parent governments, have boycotted certain trade and other commercial deals with the Soviet Union.[12]

When the Soviet grain failure of 1975 led to huge purchases of grain from the United States, the latter was anxious to link Soviet oil with grain. The Soviets wanted to separate the transaction, but unofficial sources soon discovered "that tankers carrying American grain to the USSR frequently returned with Soviet oil."[13] While the Soviets were importing American grain at the existing market price, the Americans wanted to buy Soviet oil at a fifteen percent discount, and so the United States demanded a price break

> ...to provide a signal to OPEC which could possibly have led to a reduction in world prices. Domestic political considerations were also evident; the government wanted to make additional oil reliance on the Soviet Union more palatable to the public by pointing to the low price tag.[14]

But the oil pact fell through—the Soviets obviously wanted a competitive world market price in order not to offend the OPEC countries by undercutting their official price level.[15] The Soviets were unable to enter into the world oil business on a greater scale because of extensive logistical and production difficulties. At the time, the Soviets were buying OPEC oil, and then selling it to Eastern Europe and some Third World countries.

The situation is somewhat different in Western Europe, which has traditionally been chronically deficient in oil production, even though Great Britain and Norway have had some success in developing the petroleum resources of the North Sea. Because Western Europe is geographically contiguous to the USSR, the Soviets are able to sell their oil there fairly easily—and do so more for commercial reasons than for any great political considerations. The Western Europeans also like the low price of Soviet oil, despite its somewhat reddish tinge.

Since oil is vital to the survival of modern civilization, all of the major oil powers indulge in politics, and the Soviets are no exception. They even resorted to military force to occupy the Romanian and Iranian oil fields during World War II. The Soviet Union has also assisted OPEC's oil nationalization plans, and even encouraged them to increase the base price of oil, which has directly benefited the USSR's foreign currency reserves.

The United States, on the other hand, has used its power and influence to pressure oil-producing countries to follow a certain political line. A recent example was the Soviet plan to build a pipeline to Germany and France to ship Soviet gas. The Reagan administration vehemently opposed this plan because the United States did not—and still does not—want its Western European allies to become reliant on large-scale supplies of Soviet gas and oil, lest they find themselves cut off, or dependent, in the event of an enregy crisis.

A cursory glance at the modern history of Soviet-American relations demonstrates that when both were faced with a common enemy, they joined hands and fought side by side. Whenever the United States became assertive, the Soviets either cooperated or at least remained silent. The 1991 Gulf War is an example of this, as the Iraqi invasion of Kuwait threatened the stability of the entire oil producing region. Viewed from this perspective, it may be said that the Soviets would probably cooperate with the Americans again, if the common enemy was an energy shortage so severe that civilization itself was threatened. Anything less than a catastrophic scenario, however, will likely be exploited by both sides for their immediate political benefits.

The Middle East

The long history of Soviet interest in the Middle East dates from the tsarist period and has continued under the Soviet regime. The historical search for warm-water, Middle Eastern ports remains active to the present day, although some analysts now doubt the Soviets' ability to achieve this goal.

Soviet interest in Middle Eastern oil dates from 1921, the year the USSR attempted to establish claims in northern Iran. Between the two world wars, the Soviet Union joined the Western powers in obtaining oil concessions in the Middle East. In 1947, Joseph Stalin exacted the promise of oil concessions in Iran as his condition for withdrawing Soviet troops from Azerbaijan.[16] But Stalin's attempt failed, mainly because of intervention by the United Nations, led by the United States and Great Britain.

Consequently, Soviet strategy in the Middle East has been mainly political rather than economic, although the potential benefits from enhanced economic relations with the principal OPEC nations are obvious. The Soviet need for inexpensive supplies of Middle East oil to help its Eastern European allies has already been discussed.

From the Arab and Iranian points of view, the economic outlets offered by the Soviet bloc are small in comparison with those of the capitalist world. Middle Eastern oil is not a question of life and death for the Soviets, as it presently is for the Western Europeans and the Japanese. Should it ever prove to be so, they would undoubtedly send their troops into Iran and the Persian Gulf.

During the last twenty-five years, the Soviet presence in the Middle East has steadily increased through diplomacy, deployment of military and naval forces, and the expansion of political influence in certain states, including several of the important oil-producing nations. In the Arab-Israeli dispute, the Soviets have taken advantage of the interminable conflict to supply arms and advisors to any Arab state that wants them. Thus far, the close relations between the USSR and its Arab client states have had little impact on the worldwide oil industry. But this could change if heavy Western dependence on Middle Eastern oil continues, as seems likely.

Soviet policy in the Middle East has provided political, military, and economic support for the Arab cause mainly for selfish reasons, to obtain as much oil as possible for its own domestic needs and those of its satellites. Traditional Soviet "friends" in the Middle East include Algeria, Libya, Iraq, Syria, and Yemen, all oil-producing countries except for the last. The Soviet Union has a larger Muslim population than any country in the Middle East; since 1979, neighboring Afghanistan had also been under direct Soviet military occupation. Relatedly, the Soviets sell oil to oil-poor Afghanistan at pre-1973 prices.

In general, Soviet policy in the Middle East first attempts to limit Western influence in the area, and second, to extend its own influence there. Soviet fortunes tend to fluctuate in counterbalance to those of the United States; when the U.S. image is tarnished, the USSR fills the gap. Conversely. the Middle East uses the Soviets as either a balancer or a crisis resolver. The very fact that an alternative to Western political, military, and economic assistance is readily available, gives the oil-producing states a tool to play one off against the other, thus obtaining maximum benefits from both superpowers. The Soviet Union, whenever possible, encourages the oil-rich nations to move against the Western oil monopolies, with the idea of gaining whatever political advantage it can milk from the situation.

The USSR first moved into the Middle Eastern political arena following World War II. Slowly and gradually, the Soviets developed extensive political and military ties with several Middle Eastern countries. The closing of the Suez Canal in 1956 temporarily impeded Soviet strategy in the area; although the Soviets themselves were not importing any oil from the Middle East, the closure of the Suez Canal created logistical problems for Soviet oil being shipped from the Black Sea to China and the Soviet Far East.[17]

The Soviets first purchased Arab oil in 1967, after signing an agreement with Algeria. This was soon followed by deals with Egypt and other Arab states. Soviet concerns in the Middle East are not so much aimed at obtaining oil itself as they are with depriving the capitalist world of as much oil as possible. Ironically, many Middle Eastern nations find their connections with the West much more lucrative and beneficial. After attacking American policy in the Middle East, one Soviet commentator wrote:

> The rationalization for U.S. policy in the Middle East is the alleged threat of a Soviet takeover of the area's oil. Imperialist spokesmen know, of course, that the USSR, a large oil exporter, has no need of Middle Eastern oil and does not take control of other people's resources in an imperialist manner.[18]

As part of its anti-Western line, the USSR has usually supported Arab nationalization of the petroleum and other industries, Arab oil embargos, and oil price increases (which benefit the Soviets directly). The more expensive oil is and the more supplies are disrupted, the greater the strategic advantage to the Soviets.

No single, simple explanation—whether in oil or elsewhere—wholly provides the key to Soviet strategy in the Middle East. Recent USSR policy changes cannot be considered except in relation to the global balance as a whole, and Soviet competition with the United States in particular. The Soviets will push into any area—the Middle East or elsewhere—where American influence is weakened. The Soviets know that American control over Middle East oil has been a key to its influence over other capitalist members of the world political system. The Soviets believe that long-term American oil hegemony not only dictates control over Middle East petroleum, but also over the foreign exchange earnings of the oil exporting countries.

The USSR makes no distinction between capitalist nations and oil companies. The oil companies, the Soviets say, earn high profits by paying lower wages to Third World workers, by selling oil at high prices, and by paying lower taxes.[19] In a statement typical of the USSR's pitch to Middle Eastern nations, one Soviet observer stated:

> The Arabs are faced with a glaring reality—money from exploitation of Arab oil and the labor of Arab workers subsequently finds its way into the pockets of the Israeli extremists. The money is used to buy phantom aircraft and other weapons for the Israeli armed forces while Israel is encouraged in its expansionist, criminal policy against the Arab countries. This is food for thought.[20]

The Soviets purchase Middle East oil not only to provide the oil nations with an alternate buyer, but also to prevent any effective Western boycott, particularly from the United States. If the oil producers are less reliant on the Western nations, they can more easily manipulate and bargain with them. With this in mind, the Soviets offer equipment, credit, and technical assistance to the Arab oil producers, as part of their general effort to use such aid as a tool to gain influence in the Middle East. Such offers of help establish the image the Soviets wish to convey, that of a Soviet people who are benevolently aiding poor, downtrodden Arabs to free themselves from exploitation by transnational oil companies of the West.

The Soviets have sufficiently large oil reserves to support the continued growth of their export market, to meet their own domestic needs, and to maintain their dominant energy role in Eastern Europe. The record of Soviet action in the Middle East shows that it will continue to search for a more solid basis for its long-term interests there. While the Soviets have not always been prudent in their political dealings with the rest of the world, they remain an attractive alternative to radical Arab groups, and even to some moderate forces who do not wish to seem too beholden to the West. The successful Soviet ensconcement in the heart of the oil world, especially at its Arabian core, has proven to be an historic turning point—one which has signaled a new direction in Arab relations with the United States and its allies.

Today a steady drop in oil production in the Soviet Union, until recently the world's largest oil producer, could create a new world oil shortage by turning the USSR into an oil importer rather than exporter. Soviet oil exports already are declining at least in part because some of the oil the Soviet Union was "exporting" actually was oil the Soviets had obtained from Iraq in exchange for military aircraft. Those shipments, however, were cut off in the fall of 1990 by the United Nations embargo on Iraqi oil.

Eastern European nations that formerly purchased oil from the Soviet Union on highly favorable terms are now forced to shop in the world oil market for two reasons: 1) the USSR has reduced the amount of oil it is willing to sell, even to COMECON members; and 2) the Soviets now require payment for oil in hard currency.

In an effort to bolster oil production and, with it, exports, the Soviets have invited U.S. and European companies to enter into joint ventures to provide the capital and technology that is needed in order to develop both existing and prospective oil fields within the Soviet Union.

VIII.

OIL HEGEMONY AND
THE INTERNATIONAL CRISIS

A series of events during the 1960s, 1970s, 1980s and early 1990s have caused scholars to reflect on and reevaluate the future direction of international relations. Considered separately, each of these events can be explained without a great deal of difficulty. Unfortunately, the scope of this study does not permit individual analysis, but will only allow an examination of the world oil crisis as a whole, together with its effects on the international political system.

Seldom has the world faced such a critical long-term problem as the energy crisis. A world which has been built on the idea of cheap, readily-available petroleum must now face the prospect of ever-increasing shortages, unless political and business leaders begin the process of developing alternative sources. The only other possibility is a serious decline in the standard of living in both the industrialized nations and the Third World, with the eventual collapse of the global economic order. The finite limit to the world's oil reserves is what drives the oil-producing countries to use petroleum as an economic and political weapon.

The implementation of the Arab oil embargoes, which were designed to force Israel to withdraw from the occupied Arab territories by putting unbearable economic pressures on its allies, can be seen in two contexts. The first is a forty-three-year-old struggle between Arabs and Jews over control of the narrow strip of fertile land now called Israel; the second is the drive by the oil-producing and exporting countries to take full advantage of a situation which they have themselves helped to create by manipulating the imbalance between supply and demand in order to force huge price increases upon the Western world.

Arab-Israeli Conflict and the Oil Weapon

Violence has been part of Arab-Jewish relations since the Arabs occupied Palestine in the seventh century B.C. Relatively recent hostilities can be traced to policies of the Ottoman pashas. Both the Turks and the British found their task of administering Palestine complicated by dissension between Muslims and Jews. With the creation of the state of Israel and the partition of Palestine by the United Nations in 1948, the Arabs were torn between pursuing the immediate destruction of the new Jewish state and participating in an internal struggle between the Arab states for preeminence in the region. When fighting broke out in 1948 between Israel and the Arabs, those nations not having a frontier contiguous with Palestine neither sent troops nor took an active part in the struggle, despite their strong rhetoric.[1] Egypt, Jordan, Iraq, and Syria were the principals in the war against the newly created state of Israel, and they were also the countries who lost the most when they were defeated by ragtag Jewish volunteers.

In 1956, when Great Britain and France attacked Egypt over the nationalization of the Suez Canal, Israel joined the struggle by invading the Sinai Desert. The neighboring Arab states ordered a general mobilization and called upon their Arab brothers to oppose Israel's attack. Although the war ended in an Egyptian military defeat, it became a moral and political victory when the British, French, and Israelis were forced to withdraw under considerable and widespread international political pressure, and the nationalization of the canal became a *fait accompli*.

The third war between the Arabs and Israelis broke out in June 1967, with the former calling for the annihilation of the Jewish state. But the Six-Day War ended again in a major Arab defeat, this time with the loss of significant territories belonging to the Arab principals.

After the immediate shock of the 1967 defeat had subsided, Egyptian President Gamal Abdel Nasser assumed that what had been lost by war could only be restored by war, and, with Soviet aid, began a massive military buildup. Nasser's successor, Anwar Sadat, declared, in a 1973 interview with *Newsweek*, that "everything in this country is now being mobilized in earnest for a resumption of the battle."[2]

The ostensible purpose of the Yom Kippur War of October 1973 was not to destroy Israel, but to retake the Arabs' occupied territory. Until 1967, the Arabs had demanded the complete dismantling of Israel. They now modified their stand and engineered the passing of United Nations Security Council Resolution 242, which called for an Israeli withdrawal from all occupied territories. The Arabs reaffirmed their promise not to "throw Israel into the sea" when the resolution for imposing the oil embargo was adopted in Kuwait. This Arab willingness to now live with a Jewish state on their borders arose not from love of Israel, but because of successive failures to regain territories either through war or diplomacy, and because of the terrible price their people have had to pay for these military and political failures.

Oil figured significantly in every Arab-Israeli war except the first. In 1948, Arab production was still a negligible factor on the world market. Iran was then the major Middle East producer. Great Britain still maintained complete control over the oil supply via the Suez Canal. In 1956, shipments through the Suez Canal to Western countries were temporarily blocked, and in 1967 the canal was closed completely.

When, in 1973, Egypt and Syria launched full-scale military attacks against the Israeli forces occupying their lands, the use of Arab oil as a weapon came fully into play with a five-month embargo of shipments to the United States and the Netherlands. A partial embargo was also in effect against other Western nations.

Most observers believe that a fifth Arab-Israeli war would precipitate an even more serious embargo and shortage than in 1973. The United States has stated that it will not permit Israel to be occupied by its neighbors. By the same token, Soviet support for the Arab cause cannot be assured. The Soviet Union reneged on its promise of support for the Arabs in 1967; again in 1973, it did not fulfill its announced intention to send volunteers to the Middle East to protect Arab interests. When the United States put its strategic forces on alert around the world, the Soviets maintained a very low profile. Similarly, in the 1991 Gulf War, the USSR supported the West's coalition forces against Iraq, essentially siding with the United States and ensuring U.N. condemnation of Saddam Hussein's occupation of Kuwait. Despite the fact that Iraq was the Soviet Union's chief ally in the Middle East, Soviet President Mikhail Gorbachev wanted to avoid war more than he wanted to assist a geopolitical ally.

The two superpowers may eventually come to terms in the new economic game now in progress in the Middle East. The industrialized nations of both East and West, together with Japan and the pre-industrialized and the non-industrialized countries of the Third World, are all vitally interested in securing long-term oil supplies at affordable prices. By imposing an embargo on a vital commodity like petroleum, the oil producing Arab nations have turned the Middle East crisis into a global trauma. Even the Communist states—the main supporters outside OPEC of oil price increases—are beginning to feel uneasy as the Soviet Union's own reserves begin to dwindle.

Diplomacy has played a role in the settlement of the Middle East crisis, particularly in producing the Egyptian-Israeli peace treaty. It can still succeed in a larger arena, provided that the Palestinians and most Arab extremists can refrain from calling for Israel's total destruction, and settle for a homeland on the West Bank of the Jordan River and/or the Gaza Strip, and provided that Israel can finally reconcile itself to a vocal and perhaps semi-autonomous Arab presence within its borders. A growing number of experts maintain that unless such an agreement is reached soon, another war in the Middle East is inevitable. One prominent pundit maintains that quiet diplomacy may be the only effective means to settle this vexatious conflict.[3] American helplessness stems both from its failure to stop oil price increases—thereby guaranteeing an uninterrupted flow of oil to the industrialized world—and from a seeming inability to capitalize on the success of Jimmy Carter's Mideast peace initiatives.

The situation in the Middle East has been described as follows:

> With the Palestinians playing a newly pivotal role in intra-Arab politics and with the Arab world as a whole seemingly convinced that oil will turn the tables on Israel, Rabat and its aftermath seem to have made a new war much more likely. It could break out in a number of ways, ranging from Arab attacks in response to Israeli rejections of demands for new withdrawal from the occupied territories to an Israeli preemptive war triggered by circumstances such as a new Arab "war of attrition," evidence of a coming Arab attack, or simply a feeling that a blow must be struck before the tables are hopelessly turned.[4]

In an atmosphere of constant Arab belligerency, Israel can also initiate a preemptive war against the Arabs, but it cannot do so without outside military and diplomatic support—that can only come from the United States. The question is: how far can American support reach when a new oil embargo begins devastating a highly dependent U.S. economy? America is faced with several unpalatable options: either support Israel uncritically, intervene directly, or take a neutral stance. American public opinion will never allow a fourth option, outright support of the Arabs. In the past, the United States has helped Israel with direct military assistance and diplomatic support. In the future, the U.S. may find itself directly involved—as it did in the 1991 Persian Gulf War—unless it begins rethinking its entire diplomatic posture.

Assuming that the United States can prevent Israel from intiating a preemptive attack against the Arabs—during the Gulf War, the Israelis did not retaliate against Iraq's Scud missile attacks, presumably under pressure from the U.S.-led coalition—the next question is whether the Arabs and the Palestinians can continue to abide Israeli occupation of the Gaza Strip, the Golan Heights, and the West Bank. The answer is no.

> Processes of modernization throughout the Arab world have considerably increased Arab abilities to fight a sustained war. And the decisive change in the economic balance between Israel and the Arab states brought about by the...increase in oil prices...has removed all resource constraints from Arab armament efforts.[5]

Psychological Underpinnings

The reason oil is again dominating the news is not because of a threat of an immediate embargo, but because of the almost continuous price hikes during the 1970s and early 1980s, and the sudden collapse of the price structure in the mid-1980s. If a permanent Arab-Israeli settlement is reached, will the price of oil decline? Probably not. But if it does, the specter of an international financial crisis would recede.

The Arab leaders have never promised specific concessions in return for a settlement of the Arab-Israeli conflict. If a settlement is reached through the efforts of the United States, the Soviet Union, or another third party, the Arabs might feel obligated to lower some prices in gratitude for assistance. We must remember, however, that intra-Arab-state politics is always impelled by the more radical Arab elements, who will always demand the complete destruction of Israel as a matter of religious necessity. Thus, unless the Arabs have made prior legal or moral commitments, they will use the issue of sovereignty and nationalism to justify whatever price level seems viable in the world at large. Historically, the oil producing Arab states have not always fulfilled even their legal obligations; rather, they have constantly violated or adjusted agreements made with the oil companies, often arbitrarily. Consequently, while the Arab-Israeli conflict will continue to remain a potential danger for years to come, not only for the world oil supply but also for the prospects of international peace, we should not look to a solution of that conflict as a panacea for solving the world energy crisis.

The Arab-Israeli conflict has created a political climate in the Third World that tends to support oil price increases, even when such increases have significantly harmed Third World economies. The revolutionary attempt by OPEC to seize control of a vital resource from the established industrialized powers, and to affect a radical redistribution of the world's wealth, has only been partially successful. Nonetheless, the political and strategic implications of the use of oil as a weapon of diplomacy must also be considered as part of the struggle for political hegemony among the various pre-industrialized nations of the world. The London-based International Institute for Strategic Studies concluded:

> This was the first time that major industrial states had to bow to pressure from pre-industrial ones....The victory upset the hierarchies of power long enjoyed, or resented, according to one's station, and opened up prospects of quite new political balances. By the same token, it was by far the biggest extension of the world's effective political arena since the Chinese Revolution.[6]

Basically, the Middle Eastern political climate has changed very little in the last two decades, except for the Camp David agreement, under which Egypt was given back the land occupied by Israel during the Arab-Israeli wars (except for the Gaza Strip). The question now is whether the Arabs can coordinate their policies sufficiently in the future to make effective use of coercive petrodiplomacy. OAPEC will attempt to persuade the target states to change their policy of support for Israel, and/or to force the United States to bring pressure to bear on Israel to change her policies regarding the Arabs. To some extent, this occurred in the late 1980s under U.S. President George Bush. The present oil glut has made this task more difficult, but the oversupply is merely temporary. More serious and more longlasting, perhaps, are the political divisions in the Arab world revealed by present market and political conditions.

Since the last embargo, the non-Arab and non-OPEC flow of oil to international markets has steadily increased. It is probable that these new petroleum sources will minimize the impact of future shortages, and thus mitigate against the political impact of any future embargoes. The Arabs may also be unable to limit oil shipments to embargoed countries, because such supplies are transported by a number of operators. Indeed, the Arabs had difficulties enforcing destination embargoes. Furthermore, consumers have adjusted to the idea of potential shortages, and will not again be taken by the surprise and shock so evident in 1973-74.

The energy crisis has brought together the separate pieces of the oil puzzle into a dramatic global collage that demands measures to assure consumers the world over of continued petroleum supplies at acceptable prices. We have been watching over the last two decades an erosion of the world's oil reserves and financial resources comparable in its potential to the Great Depression of the 1930s.

Whatever the overall effect of these developments, the threat of another oil embargo hangs over the world until the Arab-Israeli conflict is settled. The use of oil as a weapon in the event of another war is almost certain. Even without war, a breakdown in negotiations, or random Israeli retaliations against Arab guerrilla camps in Lebanon or elsewhere, could easily trigger another oil embargo without warning. With nearly one-third of world oil exports currently deriving from the Arab world, it is obvious that all oil importing countries have a vital interest in a settlement of major Middle East conflicts.

The International Energy Agency

How effective another oil embargo would be is difficult to predict. Several recent developments have made the task of soothsayers considerably more difficult. First, the Arab oil states are much richer now than they were in the early 1970s, so they can bear the economic cost of an embargo much longer. Second, the International Energy Agency (IEA), formed at the height of the energy crisis by all the major industrialized nations except France, has developed an elaborate self-triggering mechanism to maintain oil reserves in the event of an embargo. Therefore, an Arab oil embargo can no longer be applied selectively. Third, the present glut in petroleum supplies would, if still present during any future embargo, remove the impact of any unilateral Arab action significantly.

The inherent insecurity in the availability and transportation of energy, and the possibilities of the financial havoc that would be caused worldwide by any significant interruption in petroleum deliveries, clearly demand a wide-ranging, coordinated program among all the oil-importing nations, particularly the major importers.

It was to cope with OPEC's monopoly that, at the height of the 1973-74 energy crisis, U.S. Secretary of State Henry Kissinger first called for joint action by the consumer nations. Thirteen foreign ministers of the major oil-importing nations met in Washington for a three-day conference to discuss future energy policies. The nations represented were Belgium, Canada, Denmark, France, Germany, Ireland, Italy, Japan, Luxembourg, the Netherlands, Norway, the United Kingdom, and the United States.

As expected, the oil-producing countries vigorously objected to the conference. The Arabs were particularly disturbed by the group's far-reaching cooperative efforts to create an international energy agency designed specifically to cope with embargoes and similar emergencies by sharing available oil resources, by reducing consumption, and by tapping known reserves on an equitable basis. The energy program elicited a very muted response from the Arab capitals.[7]

The conference agreed to establish a coordinating group to direct and coordinate joint energy actions. France dissented, as it saw the American-initiated conference as a device by which it could reassert its economic domination of Europe.

Kissinger told the United Nations General Assembly that the nations of the world had been using "old patterns of thought and action"[8] to meet the new political and economic problems—the obvious insinuation being that the oil producers were taking revenge on Europe for its past colonial sins.

Ultimately, what emerged from the meeting was a four-point program of international cooperation that Kissinger hoped would avert disruptions of the Western and Japanese economies. The United States, Canada, Japan, Turkey, and twelve European countries formally created the IEA in an agreement which: (1) established an energy-sharing arrangement between the major consumers during any future embargo; (2) established cooperative conservation and energy-development programs; (3) set aside twenty-five billion dollars to recycle petrodollars into energy-deficit countries; and (4) organized a major meeting between producer and consumer countries.[9] Abstaining from the vote were France, Greece, and Finland; the five other members of the twenty-four-nation OECD voted in favor of creating the IEA, but did not join it.[10] The IEA was put under the umbrella of the Organization for Economic Cooperation and Development (OECD).

Energy-sharing, stockpiling, and conservation programs are already a part of IEA and many of its member states. A recycling account was established by the International Monetary Fund. Such mutually advantageous cooperation by oil consumers obviously implies direct confrontation with the producers. The United States has already confronted OPEC rhetorically. Proud of his role in organizing the consumer nations, U.S. Secretary of State Kissinger, said, "The United States will never permit itself to be held hostage, politically or economically."[11] While the major oil consumers were demonstrating their unity by evolving an emergency program of petroleum sharing, OPEC, in demonstration of its own unity, increased oil prices. Round two, however, went to the consumer world when the oil glut of the mid-1980s drove prices lower and seriously damaged OPEC's unity.

The battle over basic oil price levels is inexorably moving oil producers and consumers toward a major confrontation. At the height of the energy crisis in the mid-1970s, the United States had developed a plan to occupy the Middle East oil fields, if that was the only way to ensure the survival of the industrialized world. In an unusually blunt interview with *Business Week*, Kissinger observed:

> I am not saying that there are no circumstances where we would not use force. But it is one thing to use it in the case of a dispute over price, it's another where there's some actual strangulation of the industrialized world.[12]

By taking the IEA partners into its confidence, the U.S. has slowly developed links between each country's economic and energy policies. If at any time in the future the situation in the Middle East deteriorates sufficiently to make the threat of war and another oil embargo inevitable, IEA members are likely to act together against the producers, including the possibility of a joint invasion of the Middle Eastern nations and their oil fields. The producing states, on the opposite side, have undoubtedly taken measures, including deliberate sabotage, to make certain that such an invasion, even if militarily successful, would still prove a fruitless exercise in political gamesmanship. One must presume, for example, that at least the Saudi fields are mined with nuclear devices designed to seed the petroleum buried there with sufficient radioactivity to render the oil unusable for centuries, if not forever.

Assertive Competition

The oil-producing nations have argued that they should be able to price their principal resource at a level high enough to finance the maximum future economic development of their states. The problems of inflation, recession, and unemployment facing most oil-importing countries in the 1970s stemmed directly from the fact that the then-current price levels gave the exporting countries a collective revenue far in excess of their ability to absorb. This surplus threatens to undermine financial stability around the world. If OPEC were to raise prices to a sufficiently high level to meet its import and internal development requirements, there would be no world oil financial crisis of the magnitude that we are facing today.

Political conflicts in the oil-rich Middle East, especially the Arab-Israeli standoff, contribute to the critical nature of the problem. The existence of the oil cartel, with its power to fix prices during shortages, has created very difficult political problems in the world. The alternatives facing the economically marginal importing countries are bleak; if they reach the borrowing limits imposed by the larger industrialized states, they then face restrictions on trade, currency depreciations, depletions of their financial reserves, bankruptcy, or mortgaging of their financial futures as they are forced to bargain with the producers.

Is a return to the old order possible? The apparent answer is probably not, in spite of the temporary oil surpluses of the 1980s. Some transfer of power has taken place, and at least some changes in the energy balance of power may prove to be permanent. The fluctuations in world oil prices during the last two decades constitute extreme actions by producers and exporters alike, combined with equally extreme responses by the consumer states.

The basis for a permanent readjustment in oil price levels must inevitably be based on the principle that, while control of individual nations over their own natural resources is unquestioned, such control must not lead to an unrestrained exercise of power. This principle is not, of course, confined solely to petroleum, but oil remains the most difficult (and the largest) supply-and-demand problem currently affecting the world.

Any permanent solution to the oil trilemma must first assure that importing countries can obtain essential imports on terms which are both affordable and economically sustainable. This must also hold true for food and other commodities which the industrialized states supply in return. If we fail to find some middle ground which will provide the basis for long-term cooperative policies between nations—exporters and importers alike—we will erode existing political systems to the point of probable disaster, with grave implications for the future stability of world order.

Clearly, there is one solution to these world problems: genuine cooperation among interdependent nations. But resurgent nationalism is pushing many states toward confrontation, making global cooperation difficult under the best of circumstances. Emotionalism, nationalism, and sentimentalism seem to be the order of the day. The forces of regionalism and transnationalism have failed, however, to shake the basic reality of nation-state dominance in the international system as it exists today. Despite its troubles, the West still dominates the world economic order. In the long-term, the increasing uncertainty, and the new assertiveness of such states as Japan, will likely forge a new alignment in international relations; in the short-term, unfortunately, we are apt to see mini-trade wars, rising protectionism, and possibly even the collapse of some Third World "basket cases." The only certainty, as we approach the twenty-first century, is that oil will inevitably become scarcer, and prices will eventually go higher.

IX.

AFTER OIL, THEN WHAT?

Americans consume a disproportionate share of the world's energy. Of the five billion people in the world, Americans comprise a mere 250 million. As former President Richard Nixon has said:

> We use 30 percent of all the energy....That isn't bad; that is good. That means that we are the richest, strongest people in the world and that we have the highest standard of living in the world. That is why we need such energy, and may it always be that way.[1]

But the rich and powerful American nation can supply only about forty percent of its own energy; the rest must come from the relatively poor and powerless OPEC nations, all of them part of the so-called "Third World." These are facts underlying the energy crisis affecting not only America but also the world as a whole.

Accordingly, it is appropriate to ask: what are the implications for U.S. policy regarding its dependency upon unreliable foreign states to supply its basic energy needs? More specifically, does America have an oil policy? The answer would seem to be that the United States does not now have any clearly identifiable basis for dealing with the oil problem. The fact that there is currently an oversupply of petroleum in the world market is largely irrelevant, since it cannot last. The U.S. is not now involved in any energy crisis of paralyzing proportions, yet, America is still an energy-deficient country, and shortages will occur if the nation overextends itself again.

The American style of living is based on a philosophy of carefree abundance, deriving from a period when energy use was actually commercially promoted. In order to secure such posterity, adequate supplies of energy, either in the form of oil or commercially viable alternatives, must be guaranteed. To lessen its dependence on foreign oil, the U.S. must: (1) develop its own natural resources to a point where they are adequate to meet its basic needs; and (2) reconcile its presently conflicting goals concerning when, how, and where to produce these resources. Despite the fact that reliance on future imports of foreign oil would appear to be more prohibitive than the future development of existing domestic resources, it is possible that the U.S. could develop both capacities at comparable and affordable levels, using the threat of domestic development and self-sufficiency to keep oil prices relatively stable.

However, the lack of any coordinated American energy policy reflects the complexity of the issues involved. The United States currently has sixty-one agencies dealing with energy issues, but no overall energy policy. The energy crisis is really a pricing crisis, for alternatives to oil exist, but each has its own problems. Despite the energy consciousness of the 1970s, which resulted in eliminating some waste and in imposing several conservation measures, in the long-term, new energy sources must be found to replace shrinking fossil fuel reserves in the United States and in the world in general. Politics aside, energy independence for America means energy independence for the world, as vast amounts of oil will be free from American demands. The United States is uniquely blessed with massive coal and slate reserves, and with immense hydroelectric, nuclear, and solar energy potential. It must take the lead if the world's economy is to continue to grow.

The Significance of Alternative Energy Sources

In 1973, an eventful year for the oil industry, the consuming countries experienced a tightening supply-and-demand spiral for petroleum products. Seventy-five percent of proven world oil reserves and more than forty-six percent of current annual supplies derive from the Middle East and North Africa. Demand for petroleum products in the industrialized states increased steadily during the 1960s, while American domestic production leveled off or even declined. The reason why the United States is less self-sustaining today than ever before lies, firstly, in the changing picture of international politics and, secondly, in the use of the oil boycott weapon to further Arab aims. In a world where the Soviets had practically no foothold in the Middle East following World War II, the United States had a leadership role thrust upon it, and the supply source of such a strategic mineral as oil was considered guaranteed. Following establishment of *détente* and a commensurate growth in Soviet influence in the Middle East, the Arabs received added encouragement to impose an oil embargo on countries which followed a pro-Israeli policy. The events of 1973-74 made the United States and the other industrialized nations of the non-Communist world immediately conscious of the potential long-term unreliability, and even unfriendliness, of the Arab states.

The oil-exporting countries of the Arab world have been worried for some time about what will happen when they finally run out of their one finite resource—oil. Some OAPEC members have rather small populations and huge accumulated cash reserves, far more than they can reasonably spend on development projects. Thus, they are able to suspend or reduce production at will, and in a crisis situation aggravate it further by embargoing supplies for political reasons. Once the oil weapon has been used successfully, there is little reason not to use it again. Speaking to the American Society of Newspaper Editors in Washington, D.C., former Saudi Oil Minister Yamani left open the possibility of a new oil embargo if peace is not achieved in the Middle East.[2] The Arab-Israeli conflict is a local political problem which, on the surface, has little or no relevance to the energy supply-and-demand situation in the outside world. But the Arabs seem determined to wield their oil weapon once again to accomplish specific political objectives. There are many temporary remedies to such actions which we will discuss later, but the ultimate solution lies in the development of alternative sources of energy.

The U.S. dollar is drained abroad by the need to purchase petroleum at inflated prices. The cost of American oil imports skyrocketed from $8.3 billion in 1973 to twenty-five billion dollars in 1974,[3] reaching three billion dollars per month by the end of that decade. Like the strength or weakness of its dollar, any economic hardship to the U.S. is soon and automatically exported to the rest of the world, which then suffers even more than the United States. The Arab embargo of 1967 did not succeed because the United States was able to resist Arab pressure, and helped its European allies by providing them with oil supplies then available in America. The same action could not be taken in the winter of 1973-74, inasmuch as the United States itself was then dependent on Arab oil for much of its own needs.

Internationally, the American dollar is more than just another national currency, serving as the medium of international exchange in much of the world's markets. Transferring too many American dollars to the oil producers is not only a long-term danger to the health of the American economy, but also a threat to the ultimate stability of the world financial structure.

The United States, the other industrialized countries, and even the developing nations, found in the Arab oil embargo an increasing danger to their economic growth and overall standard of living. For reasons of national security, the U.S. is particularly alarmed by its growing dependence upon imported oil, which may always be subject to manipulation for political purposes. The Arab oil embargo has provided the United States with the impetus it needs to muster public support for its alternative energy development programs. The U.S. must begin a united and vigorous research and development effort into alternative energy sources. It alone has the technology and resources to do this, and there is no reason, given sufficient time and money, that such sources cannot be developed. United States energy self-sufficiency is important not only to prevent future oil embargoes, but also to save the Third World nations from ultimate economic collapse. Unfortunately, the Republican administration of Ronald Reagan abandoned many of the initiatives started by Democratic President Jimmy Carter, and adopted a head-in-the-sand attitude regarding energy development, apparently believing the oil glut would last forever. Future historians will, we believe, judge Reagan harshly for failing to use this interim grace period to reestablish U.S. energy supremacy, or at least to take the initial steps which might result in a long-term reduction of American energy dependency.

More recently, the Bush administration's national energy strategy, as presented to Congress in February 1991, called for legislation that would open the Artic National Wildlife Refuge to oil exploration and drilling, encourage the use of nuclear and other alternative energy sources, restructure the nation's vehicle fleets in order to use fuels other than gasoline, and support an increase in offshore drilling.

The post-embargo period has set the oil-importing nations upon a collision course with rising internal energy demands. Indeed, the price increases of the 1970s may have been a blessing in disguise, making many alternative energy sources directly competitive with petroleum. The collapse of petroleum price levels in the 1980s has unfortunately reversed the situation. But, judging from the suffering that the industrial world experienced in the post-embargo years, a complete reversal of the process is not expected—some development has continued. However, if the oil-exporting nations, after accumulating huge sums of American dollars, decide to flood the market to make substitute energy sources less attractive, the industrialized world could very well fall once more into the trap of consuming more than it produces. Should this happen, the consequences could be devastating for the entire world, particularly when oil resources have been depleted. An energy doomsday scenario could then ensue, followed either by World War III or a complete collapse of the world economic order. To prevent this *Götterdämmerung*, the oil-exporting nations would do well not to reduce the price of oil much below its current levels; they should also be investing their petrodollars in the development of alternative sources of energy in the West.

It is appropriate at this point to evaluate the economic and political factors which will likely play a part in determining the present and future sources of energy alternatives in the world. Technological developments may directly affect energy consumption, both by reducing production and transportation costs for primary energy sources, and by simplifying their transformation into secondary energy. The process of alternative energy development is complex, since it can be derived from coal, petroleum, gas, oil, shale, tar sand, hydropower, nuclear energy, and uranium, plus geothermal, solar, tidal, wind, and many other hitherto explored and unexplored sources of both conventional and unconventional energy.

Under normal conditions, one would expect that, as oil and gas prices increased in proportion to their relative scarcity, the more abundant and less developed fuels will appear in the marketplace as substitutes. But the approach, to date, which has focused on achieving a commercial viability for liquid fuels derived from shale, waste, or other sources, as direct replacements for crude, has met with only slight success for a number of reasons.

Particularly since the Suez crisis of 1956, the governments of the oil-importing countries have ignored the problems posed by the vulnerability of their oil supply sources. The United States, which supplied oil to Western Europe during the 1967 Arab-Israeli War, found itself unable to do so during the 1973-74 oil embargo. Project Independence was intended to provide a framework for a massive effort by the U.S. government to develop a national energy policy that would free American consumers from heavy dependence on foreign oil suppliers. This program would eliminate oil imports by developing energy substitutes and by expanding American efforts to find and recover new sources of domestic oil. Project Interdependence, on the other hand, implies energy sharing, stockpiling, conservation, international financial cooperation, and research and development through the collective efforts of the members of the International Energy Agency (IEA), founded in 1974 at the initiative of the United States. The IEA includes almost all of the Western industrialized nations plus Japan. A plan for energy independence, or for Project Interdependence, based in the first instance on American national interests, would be an essential ingredient in any new approach by the entire world to the energy situation. These projects "could make a vast difference to international relations in the next ten-to-twenty years, and serve as a step toward a more rational world use of energy for the benefit of man."[4]

Short-Term Measures

Although many short-term measures have been offered as viable alternatives to Arab oil, only the most feasible will be reviewed here. The oil glut has not changed the basic facts. The flow of Alaskan oil, for example, has not freed the United States from its continuing need for overseas supplies to meet the shortfall in its domestic market. Great Britain and Norway are extracting oil from the North Sea, and while they are virtually self-sufficient, and even able to sell their petroleum to outsiders, their reserves are projected to be depleted by the end of the century. The United States could immediately expand its domestic supplies by increasing the capacity of the Alaskan pipeline, and by opening the Navy's petroleum reserves in California and Alaska. Alaska's north slope, known as Naval Petroleum Reserve No. 4, is believed to contain as much as thirty-three billion barrels of oil.[5]

The United States could encourage more offshore domestic drilling—and has under President George Bush—and help enhance the exploration, production, and utilization of oil resources in other parts of the world. The prospect for discovering large new fields in fuel-deficient areas of the world is not great, but, should it occur, it might well alter the future global energy picture.

The stockpiling of petroleum reserves and conservation programs are essential measures to avoid future political blackmailing by OPEC and OAPEC. Simultaneously, we must try to maintain widely diversified sources of foreign oil to minimize the impact of cut-offs by one country or group of countries. During crisis periods, pollution standards may have to be lowered, including the elimination or reduction of pollution-control devices on automobiles (which directly affect mileage). While no dramatic breakthrough can be expected in automobile performance, a combination of strategies including an enforced national maximum speed limit of fifty-five miles per hour, reductions in the physical size of cars, imposition of engine-control devices to prevent acceleration above seventy-five miles per hour, introduction of electronic transportation and hydrogen fuel, could together reduce gasoline consumption significantly in the United States and abroad.

Energy experts at the Massachusetts Institute of Technology have recommended that the United States build its reserves of crude oil to offset future oil embargoes, stating that a combination of stockpiling and other measures is the best way to reduce potential risks.[6] Since their report was published in 1974, the United States has adopted such a program, securing additional supplies both from Mexico and from Iran (1.8 million barrels).[7]

TABLE 9

World Oil Consumption & Production, Base Case, 1980-2010
(Millions of barrels per day, with projections from 1990-2010)

Country	1980	1985	1990	1995	2000	2010
Market Economies: Production						
United States	10.81	11.19	9.71	8.97	8.71	7.83
Canada	1.80	1.85	1.96	2.03	2.10	2.10
OECD Europe	2.75	4.25	4.96	5.29	5.16	4.44
OPEC	27.80	17.55	23.68	26.58	28.47	34.05
Others	6.45	9.51	10.67	11.06	10.73	10.37
CPE Exports	1.24	1.96	2.20	1.92	1.53	-0.07
Net Stock Withdrawals						
United States	-0.14	0.10	-0.05	-0.04	0.03	0.01
Others	-1.35	0.27	-0.40	0.00	0.00	0.00
Total Supply	49.36	46.68	52.73	55.80	56.72	58.73
Consumption						
United States	17.45	16.00	17.61	18.42	19.06	20.55
Canada	1.87	1.50	1.68	1.91	1.96	1.90
Japan	4.96	4.38	5.20	5.77	5.65	5.02
Australia/N.Z.	0.68	0.70	0.81	0.88	0.91	1.00
OECD Europe	13.63	11.68	12.70	12.92	12.43	11.82
Others	11.07	12.82	15.02	16.21	17.01	18.75
Total Consumption	49.66	46.68	53.03	56.10	57.02	59.03
Discrepancy	0.30	0.00	0.29	0.30	0.30	0.30
Centrally Planned Economies: Production						
China	2.11	2.51	2.81	2.82	2.77	2.50
Soviet Union	11.99	11.99	12.03	11.56	10.48	8.16
Others	0.46	0.48	0.51	0.42	0.35	0.24
Consumption						
China	1.77	1.78	2.12	2.11	2.09	2.02
Soviet Union	9.00	8.95	8.82	8.50	7.88	7.06
Others	2.71	2.53	2.40	2.28	2.10	1.89
World Oil Consumption	63.14	59.94	66.37	68.99	69.09	70.00

Sources: *International Energy Annual 1988, Monthly Energy Review 1989, Quarterly Oil Statistics* (International Energy Agency), *Quarterly Supply/Demand Outlook* (Petroleum Economics Ltd.), *Oil Market Simulation Model* (Energy Information Administration).

Furthermore, as a response to the potential disruption of oil imports, the United States has supplemented the nation's energy supplies by purchasing a large amount of crude oil for stockpiling in the U.S. Strategic Petroleum Reserve (SPR). Over 600 million barrels are currently stored—in contrast to only ninety-one million barrels in 1979. Under the current policy, the SPR is scheduled to reach 780 million barrels by the end of 1991. While the bulk of these oil reserves was purchased from Mexico, smaller quantities were purchased from Great Britain, Norway, and Saudi Arabia. As a test case, the Bush administration released five million barrels of SPR oil to the open market in order to keep the price of oil down during the Persian Gulf War.

Should a major disruption in oil supplies occur once again, the United States and its OECD allies have developed plans to coordinate the early use of government-controlled stocks to mitigate any adverse economic effects. At the end of 1989, the major oil-consuming nations owned stockpiles of nearly one billion barrels of oil. Currently, these government-owned reserves can provide the U.S. and its allies with a potential six-month supply of oil to cushion any disruption in oil shipments similar to those experienced in the 1970s.

Stockpiling has also been successfully used by European countries. The size of an effective reserve depends directly upon the magnitude of the expected embargo, but stockpiling a year's consumption of foreign oil may be enough to cushion the shock of a future emergency. A reserve of about one billion barrels would permit America to draw three million barrels a day for one year in case of another embargo—the U.S. reserve is presently just over half that amount.

Many studies have been published showing that the United States can cut back its oil consumption by two and one-half million barrels a day (more than fifteen percent) without hardship.[8] The Ford Foundation's four million dollar inquiry into the American energy crisis, whose authors included leading economists, lawyers, and scientists, maintains that the United States can balance its energy needs and avoid reliance on potentially unreliable foreign oil sources by slowing the growth rate of domestic energy consumption.[9] The authors assert that American energy growth can be trimmed to about two percent a year, or perhaps even to zero, without adversely affecting the economy.[10]

It was because of conservation measures that oil consumption fell drastically in the first half of 1974 in the European Common Market countries. Compared with the first six months of 1973, oil use fell by fifteen and one-half percent in [West] Germany, 9.9 percent in Great Britain, and 6.1 percent in France. Consumption dropped even more in some of the smaller countries—22.8 percent in the Netherlands, 19.1 percent in Belgium, 15.7 percent in Denmark, and sixteen percent in Luxembourg.[11]

While stockpiling and conservation measures should go hand in hand, the United States must also attempt to diversify its foreign sources of oil. Production of domestic petroleum products should also be increased. Unfortunately, American oil production has actually declined in recent years, mainly due to the oil glut of the mid-1980s, which has made oil exploration unprofitable for the large petroleum companies.

New Energy Sources

Possible timetables for the availability of alternate energy sources vary considerably from expert to expert. Most concede, however, that there are three elements integral to any time line that might be devised: the political, economic, and technological. Disagreement is narrowing, and a convergence of opinion concerning what is technically feasible is emerging, as is some consensus regarding what should receive high-level political and economic support. Presidents Ford, Carter, Reagan, and Bush have, in their energy messages to the American people, suggested that such a convergence may well have arrived. The serious tenor of these messages emphasizes that the era of cheap energy is gone, perhaps forever. Despite the fact that the price of oil fell in the mid-1980s (although not as much as it should have, given the market price of crude), and that OPEC nearly collapsed, and increasing pressures for more production by both member states (particularly Iran and Iraq) and non-OPEC nations, never again will the price of petroleum be as low as it was in 1973. In a sense, higher oil prices are essential to develop alternate and renewable sources of energy; otherwise the world will continue to be utterly dependent on cheap—but nonrenewable—oil.

Any reasonable assessment of alternative energy sources must include, on a short-term basis, the production of electricity by nuclear power plants. Although some sixty scientists concluded in a study done for the Atomic Energy Commission that concerns about nuclear danger had been vastly exaggerated,[12] the disaster at Chernobyl in the Soviet Union has raised new questions about the long-term viablity of the industry. Even if the safety issues are settled, the question of what to do with the radioactive wastes, or even with the plants themselves, is one which has not been well-addressed by the industry.

The social costs of nuclear power have been the subject of considerable debate; the U.S. government has itself invested more than one billion dollars in attempts to measure the environmental and societal costs associated with nuclear power.[13] As a result, a vast amount of literature has fueled the public debate over potential nuclear hazards. The debate has often been unbalanced in light of the absence of any readily available substitute for the limited reserves of fossil fuels. The issue is likely to remain unresolved as more studies on the danger of nuclear fuels appear, and since we cannot effectively do without them unless we wish to see an immediate drop in our standard of living. In 1974, David J. Rose, a nuclear scientist, concluded:

> The uranium and thorium resources, the technology and the
> societal impacts all seem to presage an even sharper increase in
> nuclear power for electric generation than hitherto has been pre-
> dicted.[14]

The National Petroleum Council also predicted that by 1985 electrical power generation from nuclear energy would have expanded to forty-two percent.[15] However, both the council and Rose failed to take into account three factors: new scientific evidence that even small amounts of radioactivity can be hazardous to human health; the increasing public perception of nuclear facilities as inherently unsafe; and staggering increases in the costs of constructing such facilities and in liability coverage for completed plants. A fourth factor has also come into play: the cost of making unsafe plants safe, and an industry-wide miscalculation in how long individual facilities can safely be used to generate power (most existing plants will have to be dismantled within forty years).

Concern over the safety of nuclear power increased considerably after the accidents at Three Mile Island and Chernobyl. Subsequently, construction of new facilities virtually stopped worldwide, except in the Soviet Union. The possibility of uranium shortages by the year 2000 must inevitably make the nuclear industry a short-lived one, unless safe breeder reactors or fusion plants can be developed. Three Mile Island represents the most serious accident to date in the history of U.S. nuclear power industry. Nuclear opponents contend that a full-fledged disaster was narrowly averted, and that the accident demonstrates the inherent dangers of nuclear power. Proponents argue that the dangers have been unduly sensationalized.

The consequences of the 1979 accident were profound. Governments the world over nervously reassessed their nuclear power plans. A United States presidential commission concluded that, although no one had been harmed, the accident was much more serious than claimed by the operators, and it recommended a restructuring of the Nuclear Regulatory Commission (NRC). Sweden scheduled a referendum on the issue, and Japan closed down its nuclear plants. Throughout the industrialized West, vocal opposition to nuclear power was expressed through intense lobbying by anti-nuclear and environmental groups. Unfortunately, there are no short-term alternatives to nuclear energy in the United States and Western Europe, and viable, long-term solutions, while technically feasible, have yet to be developed at commercial prices. The time to begin such projects is now, before new oil shortages develop, and while nuclear facilities can still make up some of the difference. Alas, we have yet to see much leadership on this issue from either the Congress or the president.

Energy Independence

An energy-autonomous United States would have the capability of countering future oil embargoes by helping the Western European nations and Japan to overcome their inherent vulnerability as neither have abundant natural energy sources of their own. An energy program can only be based on a combination of nuclear, solar, and tidal power development, since the European continent generally lacks petroleum resources, except in the North Sea region (and these are very limited). The American reorganization of the Atomic Energy Commission (AEC) under two new agencies—the Energy Research and Development Administration (ERDA) and the NRC—represents a step in the right direction. We must find better ways to develop a safe nuclear alternative and to re-establish public confidence. It is here that nations on both sides of the Atlantic can cooperate to meet seemingly insurmountable technical problems. West European nations, including "pro-Arab" France, are drawing closer to the United States on energy matters. Japan, although a developed nation, is physically located in the less-developed region of the world. Yet, Japan must also move closer to the United States in order to secure its energy future.

Historically, America's capacity for innovation in energy technology has been unsurpassed: oil was first drilled and exploited on a large-scale basis in the United States; the large-scale use of coal and steam to operate factories and trains was also an American first.

TABLE 10

World Net Nuclear Electric Power Generation, 1980-1988¶
(Quadrillion (10^{15}) Btu)

Region/Country	1980	1981	1982	1983	1984	1985	1986	1987	1988§
Americas									
Argentina	.03	.03.	.02	.04	.05	.06	.06	.07	.06
Brazil	.00	.00	*	*	.02	.03	*	.01	*
Canada	0.42	0.44	0.42	0.54	0.57	0.66	0.78	0.84	0.90
U.S.A.	2.74	3.01	3.13	3.20	3.55	4.15	4.47	4.91	5.68
Total	3.19	3.48	3.57	3.78	4.19	4.91	5.32	5.83	6.64
Western Europe									
Belgium	.12	.13	.15	.24	.28	.34	.39	.41	.42
Finland	.07	.14	.16	.17	.18	.18	.18	.19	.19
France	.72	1.02	1.06	1.40	1.87	2.15	2.43	2.53	2.64
F.R.G.	.46	.56	.67	.69	.97	1.31	1.24	1.36	1.43
Italy	.03	.03	.08	.07	.08	.08	.10	*	.00
Holland	.04	.04	.04	.04	.04	.04	.04	.04	.04
Spain	.06	.11	.10	.12	.25	.30	.40	.44	.52
Sweden	.26	.36	.37	.39	.49	.56	.67	.64	.66
Switz.	.14	.14	.14	.15	.17	.21	.21	.22	.23
U.K.	.42	.43	.50	.57	.58	.64	.62	.57	.66
Yugo.	.00	*	.03	.04	.05	.05	.05	.05	.04
Total	2.31	2.96	3.30	3.87	4.96	5.86	6.34	6.46	6.83
Eastern Europe and the Soviet Union									
Bulgaria	.06	.10	.11	.13	.13	.14	.13	.13	.13
Czech.	.05	.05	.07	.07	.08	.14	.21	.26	.26
G.D.R.	.13	.13	.12	.13	.13	.14	.12	.12	.12
Hungary	.00	.00	.00	.03	.04	.07	.08	.12	.14
USSR	.79	.73	.86	1.19	1.53	1.81	1.74	2.00	2.32
Total	1.03	1.01	1.16	1.54	1.92	2.29	2.27	2.63	2.97
Middle East	.00	.00	.00	.00	.00	.00	.00	.00	.00
Africa									
S.Africa	.00	.00	.00	.00	.04	.06	.09	.06	.11
Total	.00	.00	.00	.00	.04	.06	.09	.06	.11
Far East & Oceania									
India	.03	.03	.02	.03	.05	.05	.06	.06	.07
Japan	.85	.85	1.06	1.11	1.29	1.54	1.67	1.89	1.75
S.Korea	.03	.03	.04	.09	.12	.17	.28	.39	.39
Pakistan	*	*	*	*	*	*	.01	*	*
Taiwan	.08	.11	.13	.19	.24	.28	.26	.33	.30
Total	.99	1.02	1.25	1.42	1.70	2.04	2.27	2.66	2.51
World Totals	7.51	8.47	9.28	10.62	12.81	15.15	16.29	17.64	19.06

¶Generation data consist of both utility and non-utility sources; §Preliminary; *Denotes less than five trillion Btu. Note: Data are reported as net generation as opposed to gross. Net generation excludes the energy consumed by the generating unit. Sum of components rounded off and may not equal totals. No production is reported for the Middle East. Source: Energy Information Administration, U.S. Department of Energy: *International Energy Annual, 1988*. Washington, D.C., 1989.

More recently, a group of American scientists has developed an engine that converts gasoline into hydrogen. Pilot studies are also being conducted to use pure hydrogen for propulsion.[18] These innovations, along with the attempt to use hydrogen for home heating and cooling, may not only bail America out of its energy shortage, but save the world from future economic peril. Hydrogen-powered automobiles may well be mass-produced by early in the twenty-first century.

Coal Is King Again

Coal is a second alternative for development as a synthetic crude oil (syncrude), or as synthetic gas (syngas); it can also be burned directly to heat homes or to drive electric power plants.

The United States has the largest proven coal reserves in the world; it provides more than one-third of all the primary energy produced in the U.S. and supplies nearly one-fourth of all energy used by Americans. Major coal fields are located across the United States and have an estimated supply-life of three hundred years. With proven oil fields fast being depleted, coal seems to hold the promise for much wider use as a fuel-based transportation system. Syncrude, syngas, and methyl alcohol (methanol) can be generated from coal, although not yet at commercially viable prices. The advantages of coal gasification and liquefaction have been aptly described by Wilson Clark:

> Besides the convenience offered by gasification and liquefaction in terms of not having to convert or replace existing fuel-burning devices to utilize them, these two related technologies also offer another attractive advantage over coal in its natural state; and that is that the pollutants—the sulfur, the nitrogen oxides, the ash, etc.—are removed in the gasification process, leaving a clean fuel. It is both cheaper and simpler to remove pollutants at this stage than try to remove them from the smokestack after coal is burned as a fuel.[19]

111

TABLE 11

World Coal Production, 1980-1988
(Quadrillion [10¹⁵] BTUs)

Country	1980	1982	1984	1986	1988
		AMERICA			
Brazil	.19	.14	.16	.17	.17
Canada	.85	.98	1.34	1.36	1.66
Chile	.02	.02	.03	.04	.08
Colombia	.13	.16	.17	.26	.38
Mexico	.14	.15	.18	.17	.19
United States	18.60	18.64	19.72	19.51	20.74
Other	.01	.02	.02	.01	.04
Total	19.94	20.11	21.61	21.53	23.26
		WESTERN EUROPE			
Austria	.04	.05	.04	.04	.03
Belgium	.16	.17	.16	.14	.13
France	.54	.51	.48	.42	.42
West Germany	3.96	4.15	3.83	3.73	3.48
Greece	.12	.14	.17	.20	.26
Italy	.02	.02	.02	.02	.02
Norway	.01	.01	.01	.01	.01
Spain	.53	.69	.71	.71	.59
Turkey	.24	.31	.49	.66	.66
United Kingdom	3.02	2.94	1.17	2.56	2.46
Yugoslavia	.55	.64	.74	.77	.78
Other	.01	.02	.01	.01	.01
Total	9.20	9.63	7.82	9.27	8.85
		EASTERN EUROPE AND U.S.S.R.			
Albania	.02	.02	.02	.03	.03
Bulgaria	.43	.45	.45	.45	.48
Czechoslovakia	1.85	1.87	1.91	1.87	1.87
East Germany	2.17	2.32	2.50	2.62	2.67
Hungary	.32	.32	.31	.28	.27
Poland	5.00	4.92	5.10	5.46	5.97
Romania	.47	.48	.58	.61	.67
Soviet Union	13.24	13.31	13.24	13.95	14.74
Total	23.50	23.71	24.11	25.27	26.70
		AFRICA			
Morocco	.02	.02	.02	.02	.02

Mozambique	.01	.02	.02	—	—
South Africa	2.72	3.23	3.82	4.16	4.15
Zambia	.01	.01	.01	.01	.01
Zimbabwe	.08	.07	.06	.10	.14
Other	.01	.02	.02	.02	.02
Total	2.85	3.37	3.94	4.30	4.35
MIDDLE EAST, FAR EAST, OCEANIA					
Australia	2.15	2.65	2.78	3.68	3.85
China	12.65	13.58	16.09	17.74	19.50
India	2.41	3.00	3.41	3.85	3.81
Indonesia	.01	.01	.03	.06	.07
Iran	.02	.02	.02	.03	.03
Japan	.44	.43	.40	.39	.25
North Korea	1.14	1.19	1.16	1.24	1.39
South Korea	.37	.36	.41	.50	.50
Mongolia	.04	.05	.06	.06	.08
New Zealand	.05	.05	.06	.05	.06
Pakistan	.03	.03	.04	.04	.06
Philippines	.01	.01	.02	.02	.02
Thailand	.01	.01	.02	.05	.07
Vietnam	.15	.14	.13	.14	.16
Other	.07	.08	.06	.05	.04
Total	19.54	21.61	24.68	27.91	29.89
World Total	75.02	78.44	82.16	88.27	93.04

Source: *International Energy Annual 1988* (Washington: U. S. Dept. of Energy, Energy Information Administration, 1989).

Although there is great uncertainty in predicting the cost of such new technology, the MIT Energy Laboratory Policy Group notes that for all processes involved, capital investment is very similar to that of the old technology.[20] The National Petroleum Council (NPC) has projected that syngas could supply two and one-half trillion cubic feet of gas per year "at the maximum rate physically possible without any restrictions due to environmental problems, economics, etc."[21]

The demand for gas in 1985 was about forty-one trillion cubic feet; the supply of domestic gas fell short of that mark by about 10 trillion cubic feet.[22] To fill this gap with syngas would require the construction of a minimum of 120 coal gasification plants, at a capital cost of some twenty-four billion dollars. As the demand for energy in general will increase, the U.S. production of domestic gas will peak to twenty trillion cubic feet by the year 2000.

Research and development for syncrude is slower than for syngas. Within ten years, the United States could have ten syncrude plants, each with a 100,000-

barrel-per-day capacity.[23] The oil shortage in the United States has sparked new interest in the technology of coal liquefaction, since coal is the largest naturally-occurring energy resource in the U.S. By producing syncrude from coal, America would suddenly find itself with a 150-year extension of its energy deadline,[24] in addition to coal's other, rather obvious uses. Oil could also be produced from huge shale deposits in the western United States, and probably from similar large tar sand reserves in Canada. But imported oil may have become worthless long before the United States runs out of coal. Taking into consideration the potential future rise in the cost of imported oil, syncrude will undoubtedly be economically competitive by the year 2000.

The editor of *Science* magazine, in an editorial published just before the 1973 embargo, urged increased federal funding for coal liquefaction:

> In comparison with the billions we spend on oil imports...the millions the government is devoting to liquefaction of coal can best be described as a phony commitment—a cosmetic effort whose purpose is to give the appearance, but not the reality, of action. A goal worthy of the world's leader in technology would be to construct in two years several plants, each costing about $1 billion and each capable of supplying 1 percent of the liquid hydrocarbons we consume.[25]

His words still hold true today, nearly two decades later.

According to Yale University economist William D. Nordhaus, the cost of continued U.S. reliance on foreign oil during the two decades from 1975 to 1995 will total some $663 billion, while the total sum needed to secure American energy independence during the same period would amount to $985 billion, a difference of just $16 billion annually.[26] This is not an impossible goal. Further exploration and development of natural gas and oil from the outer continental shelf will not cut oil imports to zero; the United States would do better by investing an additional sixteen billion dollars annually to achieve the overall energy autonomy so necessary to maintain its high standard of living.

Coal was king in the nineteenth century, and it remains an old, reliable, abundant source of energy for the United States. Syngas was once widely used in the United States,[27] until about 1955, when American utilities shifted from syngas to natural gas. The process can be reversed without hardship to the economy or to consumers. Similarly, a new technology to develop syncrude can be made to function without major hardship—if the investment is begun now.

The energy problems facing the world in general, and the United States in particular, do not require exploitation of every energy source, since there are still many which are amenable to a technological solution. Efforts must concentrate on the most feasible of these—technologically, financially, politically, and environmentally. Several forms of energy are eternal in nature, including solar power and geothermal resources. Of these, we will artificially exclude geothermal energy, since the simultaneous development of two parallel eternal sources of energy is a financially unsound proposition. Geothermal resources are highly localized, and cannot possibly provide the basis for a centralized, national energy system. Moreover, "theoretically, as the earth's heat is converted into electrical power, the total heat in the earth would drop."[28] Thus, in the strictest sense, the only inexhaustible primary source of energy is that radiated from the sun. (For purposes of this discussion, we shall consider tidal and wind power as other aspects of solar energy.)

Solar Energy

Scientists and engineers across the world have begun converting solar energy into heat, electricity, or even chemical fuels:

> Within five years, many of these scientists believe solar-powered systems for heating and cooling homes could be commercially available at prices competitive with gas or oil furnaces and electric air conditioners. More significant, but farther in the future, is using heat from the sun to generate electricity; experimental solar-thermal generators have been constructed in several countries, and several groups in the United States are designing systems that take advantage of improved materials and manufacturing techniques. Eventually the direct conversion of solar radiation to electricity by means of photovoltaic cells or its bioconversion to wood, methane, or other fuels on a large scale may become economically feasible.[29]

Solar water heaters have been in commercial use in California and Florida since the 1930s.[30] They are also in use in many European countries, and in Japan, the Soviet Union, Australia, and Israel. The heating and cooling of buildings by the sun's radiation is a practical economic probability,[31] and its widespread future use in homes is inevitable by the year 2000.[32] Solar radiation is so abundant that the energy arriving from the sun on just one-half of one percent of the total land area in the United States is more than enough to meet America's entire energy requirement by the year 2000.[33]

Because of the cost of installing solar systems in existing homes that were never designed for them, and because of the slow rate of replacing such existing residences, solar technology will take at least several decades before it has any significant impact on energy useage. The Ford Foundation's Energy Policy Project estimates that it would take a half-century for the impact of solar energy on society to be felt, by which time new housing would replace most existing homes.[34] Scientists at the American Association for the Advancement of Science feel that because of the growing shortage of fossil fuels, solar energy will be widely used within the next several decades.[35] As society begins to realize that cheap fossil fuels are not easily available, scientists have suggested that collection of solar energy on house rooftops may be commercially feasible. This process is already used sporadically in the sunbelt of the United States. Its widespread use in existing homes is a viable possibility as conventional energy sources dwindle and as the political climate hitherto inimical to the development of solar energy disappears. Interest in the large-scale application of solar energy has accelerated in the United States and presidents from Nixon to Bush have issued messages suggesting the need for the further development of the sun's energy.

But is it worth the effort? The answer must be yes. A number of corporations—large and small—have started research projects in this, including Shell, Mobil, Boeing, ARCO, Union Carbide, Varian, Solarex, Ametex, and many others. The U.S. Congress, with the passage of the Photovoltaic Act of 1978, set a target research grant of one and one-half billion dollars over ten years. Some 450 solar projects had received federal grants by 1980. While solar energy remains a more expensive alternative to oil, increasing costs of conventional energy sources will eventually make its collection much more attractive. The high costs of converting solar energy to usable forms can be reduced through advanced technology and mass production. As George Lof has stated:

> In favorable locations, the costs of solar heating and cooling equipment under development appear to be nearly competitive with fuels; hence, this application is expected to be widespread within a very few years. Electric power from solar energy is not now competitive with conventional supply and is, therefore, a longer term possibility.[36]

Expert opinion holds that the development of a competitive solar electricity industry in the United States will take several decades, but such development is essential as a supplemental source of energy, particularly in the sun-rich but water-poor Southwest. The development of efficient solar heating and cooling facilities by 1995 is a practical and realistic projection, if government provides the proper support in the form of financial incentives and tax breaks. By the time the new century dawns, solar housing may add a new chapter to the lifestyle of twenty-first-century man.

In summary, we can say that oil will surely maintain its favored position as the primary source of man's energy requirements, probably until the end of this century, and will decline progressively thereafter. However, the crucial period for its replacement is *now*. We must begin preparing for a steady shift away from oil and toward the use of nuclear, coal, and solar energy. If we fail to do this, we will doom our own civilization to extinction.

In looking at the real technological and economic possibilities of the various alternative sources of energy now available, we can see that only nuclear fission, coal gasification and liquefaction, and solar energy seem immediately attainable substitutes. "We should expect to be using an energy mix, just as we do now, with each energy source supplying the requirements which it can satisfy in the most suitable way...."[37]

Each of the other alternatives to fossil fuels has its problems. Oil shale has been mentioned as an especially attractive possibility, since there are large deposits in the western United States. However, shale mining is expensive, destructive to large segments of the environment, and leaves large mounds of shale tailings after the oil is extracted. Another problem is that shale crude must be further treated to improve its quality to commercial levels; this process in itself requires more energy. The main pilot project, on the Utah-Colorado border, was shut down when the U.S. government withdrew its support. Tar sands, another alternative often mentioned, are located in commercial quantities only in Canada, an increasingly fickle ally.

Man's energy problem is global in nature, and its solution will require co-operation from both producers and consumers. America, as usual, must lead the way to energy independence. Failure to do so may result in calamity as mankind enters the twenty-first century—if not sooner.

X.

CONCLUSIONS

OAPEC's decision to impose an oil embargo in 1973 immediately cata-pulted the parent organization into a position of great power. OPEC suddenly found itself able to command oil prices higher than anyone had ever thought possi-ble. Both Arab and non-Arab members alike supported the price revolution by us-ing petroleum as a politically motivated weapon against the United States and other supporters of Israel. But even after the embargo ended, production and pricing de-cisions remained with OPEC.

Three oil regimes have dominated world politics. The first did not rec-oncile the oil interests of consumers and producers, but did manage to secure the interests of the industrialized nations well enough to provide a remarkably durable industrial base. The second oil regime gave the world low prices and increasing supplies, allowing the industrialized West to expand dramatically following World War II. The third oil regime began with the 1973 embargo. The confrontation between the Middle East and the West is likely to continue, despite the recent drop in oil prices, until diversified sources of energy are developed by the West, and un-til oil itself is replaced as a vital commodity.

The third regime is dominated by three nations: the United States, as the largest consumer; Saudi Arabia, as the largest non-Communist producer; and hith-erto the Soviet Union, as the largest producer in the world. In the event of a new oil crisis, the Soviets may exploit its huge oil reserves by increased sales to favored nations. The Soviets may also be willing to sell or exchange their oil for American food and high technology. Another new development prompted by OPEC's high price levels is the attempt to increase oil production by non-OPEC nations. A sig-nificant development in this regard has been the growing importance to the United States of Mexico as a producer and exporter of oil and gas. Increased Mexican sales to the U.S. will ultimately lessen American dependence upon OPEC nations.

As more diversification of oil sources has taken place, prices have fallen, the political power of OPEC has weakened, and the potential use of oil as a weapon or political instrument by a single group has been minimized, at least in the short term. In the long term, unless America makes a real effort to develop alternate sources of energy, another embargo of the magnitude of 1973 will remain a real possibility.

The International Energy Agency, made up primarily of the industrialized Western nations, is attempting to store up oil stocks sufficient to withstand a six-month supply disruption. The U.S. government has itself taken similar measures.

These supplies provide a certain measure of independence for the industrialized world from OPEC's oil-based rule. Also, internal political conflicts within OPEC during the 1980s have weakened its power to deal effectively with petroleum pricing levels, as individual member states have consistently violated production limits set by the group as a whole. The revolution in Iran, the Iran-Iraq War, and the Gulf War have further complicated uniform decision-making efforts by OPEC.

Some small shifts in Western energy policies away from total reliance upon oil have improved the situation, but many of these have unfortunately been abandoned or cut back in the last few years. For almost a decade, it was unthinkable to build new oil-fired electric generators, for example, and many older ones were converted to coal. Under the Reagan administration, many of the support programs designed to wean America from its oil habit were allowed to lapse. Long-term plans to reduce American dependence on petroleum must soon be implemented if they are to have any effect by the time the next shortage occurs. Needless to say, the survival of modern civilization depends on the joint success of developing alternatives to oil. A new energy consciousness must be raised in order to reduce substantially the West's use of petroleum-based products.

Uncertainties continue to exist regarding both future demands for oil and the terms upon which this oil will be supplied. These, in turn, depend somewhat on the rate of growth of the world economy and the industrialized world's reaction to future high oil prices.

As production capacity increased throughout the world in the 1980s and demand decreased, oil prices dropped. For obvious reasons, consumers prefer these lower levels and will undoubtedly resist deliberate attempts to keep them higher. But energy independence may first require higher price levels to provide us with the needed incentives to diversify. The abundant availability of alternate energy resources, subject to technical feasibility and economic competitiveness, should in the long run provide sufficient energy to meet the world's needs.

A drive toward world energy self-sufficiency, centering on conservation, the recovery of oil from onshore and offshore areas, and the development of various alternative sources of energy, would go a long way toward reducing America's dependency on imported oil. In the meantime, if another Arab-Israeli war should break out, the Arabs can be expected to use their oil weapon again, for whatever political advantage they can gain. In practice, another embargo might result in more dangerous consequences for the Arabs themselves, as the non-OPEC nations, including the Soviet Union, could very easily make up the difference, if they so chose. Selective embargoes against the United States would have little chance of success. Moreover, a total embargo against the non-Communist industrialized nations might well be met by a military response from the West, including occupation of selected oil fields by American or allied troops. Therefore, Arab petrolism as a political weapon, unless carefully applied, has only minimal chances of success.

The Soviet Union, as a geographical neighbor of the Middle East, is very concerned with that part of the world. Over the long term, the USSR has proven itself a more reliable business partner in its dealings with the West than have the volatile OPEC nations. We must understand, however, that the Soviet Union would not stand idly by if its allies in the Middle East were invaded by the Western powers, and that distances, logistics, and military factors suggest that the Soviet Union is still capable of quickly launching a conventional war to ensure the success of its policy in the Middle East.

The essence of Soviet policy in the Middle East is geopolitical as well as military. If the Soviets are satisfied that their political interests would not be served by intervening, they would not block United States forces from taking control of the region's oil wealth. It is one thing for the Soviets to occupy Afghanistan, but it is quite another to risk total war through a direct confrontation with American troops.

The Arabs hoped—and the Israelis feared—that the 1973 oil embargo would bring about a quick settlement of the Arab-Israeli conflict. Undoubtedly, some progress was made toward disengagement and the speedy pullback of Israeli troops from some occupied areas, but the embargo itself quickly transferred a regional conflict into a global energy and financial crisis.

The most obvious long-term consequence of high-priced oil is a massive redistribution of the world's wealth. While the industrial countries may sink into recession, the oil-producing states may suddenly be glutted with bullion and dollars. The higher prices were in effect for nearly a decade, before the pricing structure collapsed in the mid-1980s. The long-term effect of high oil prices is an immense balance of payments problem in the Third World and in the United States. Oil import deficits in the industrialized nations ran about $50 billion a year during the 1970s, and about $70 billion in the Third World. The industrialized economies can often absorb this deficit, but the less developed countries keep piling up their debt burden.

With this great transfer of wealth to the Arab states, particularly Saudi Arabia, a subtle shift in power has also taken place. Not only do the major oil-producing states control a vital resource without which the Western countries cannot survive, but they have also accumulated huge financial reserves and assets, which they have invested back into the industrialized economies. In the case of future international conflicts, these investment assets could be withdrawn by the OPEC nations in order to destabilize national currencies or to deliberately weaken the economies of those nations that fail to support their policies.

The damage that higher oil prices have done to Western economies handicaps them against the Soviet Union in the arms race and other areas. This works against the long-term interests of the Saudi Arabian monarchy, which depends on Western protection against communism and internal political subversion. The social discontent fostered by the prospects of continuing cycles of recession, inflation, and high unemployment, together with a declining standard of living, may eventually fuel authoritarian forms of government in the industrial West. In the Third World, governments struggling against ever-worsening economic conditions will become more authoritarian, dictatorial, and repressive. Their leaders will discover that an aggressively assertive foreign policy is one means to divert people from their domestic problems by providing them with foreign scapegoats. A rising level of world tension is the inevitable outcome of such policies.

The 1973 oil embargo, and the price increases which accompanied it, hurt the undeveloped nations of the Third World more than it did the industrialized countries of the First World. OPEC, however, has since alleviated that predicament somewhat by setting aside a share of its windfall profits from oil to help support the Third World's balance of payment problems, to help finance industrial projects, to provide general financial assistance and jobs, and to support energy and food production in the Third World.

In summary, our major conclusions are: 1) although oil may still be a vital commodity, the need for developing alternative sources of energy and new technology is great and immediate; 2) the industrialized West must stockpile oil to avoid OPEC blackmailing; 3) energy conservation must be pursued at all levels; 4) particular emphasis must be placed in the United States on developing its large coal reserves; 5) additional research and international action are needed to develop nuclear energy, particularly breeder reactors and nuclear fusion; and 6) further efforts must be directed toward the development of a viable solar energy industry.

Ultimately, another oil embargo like that of 1973 would be economically disastrous for producer and consumer countries alike. OPEC countries can no longer realistically afford to raise their petroleum prices indiscriminately without hurting more and more of their friends, the oil-less Third World countries, particularly those in their own region. Oil will play an insignificant role in the Arab attempt to settle their differences with Israel. Finally, oil prices will always be subject to manipulation by OPEC, but prices may no longer rise or drop significantly solely due to OPEC's wishes or actions. OPEC itself may fragment as intra-Arab squabbles intensify. The West, however, should not put much faith in such Polly Annish dreams as again restoring hegemony over this part of the world.

Our final conclusion is thus inevitable. In both the near and distant future, no firm reliance can be placed on the availability of OPEC oil at inexpensive or even "acceptable" prices. The experience of the early 1970s should have taught American consumers this lesson, but it has evidently failed to do so. Unless the United States reforms its profligate ways, the economic future of both the U.S. and its Western allies is grim indeed. The choice is simple: we can pay now, and introduce some manageable sanity into our economic future—or we can pay a great deal more later, at a perhaps unbearable price.

XI.

POSTSCRIPT

The winds of change which have buffetted the energy scene over the past two decades have had profound effects on the world economic and political outlook. The years from 1973 to 1986 witnessed an extraordinary rise in the economic power of a group of heretofore indigent nations; these oil-exporting countries have gradually seized control of the international oil companies and dictated the price of oil. The major concern in the 1970s was that skyrocketing oil prices would bring on a worldwide recession, and they did, indeed, help to do just that. Ironically, the opposite fear existed in the 1980s: declining oil prices. This caused difficulty, too, when some oil-producing countries and many Third World nations were forced to default on their debts. Now—in the 1990s—supplies of energy are clearly abundant and prices are relatively low; however, emerging trends are raising serious concerns.

When oil prices fell precipitously during 1986, the decline brought good economic news to both oil consumers and to users of all forms of energy. Partly as a consequence of lower oil prices, however, the world as a whole turned again toward countries in the historically unstable Persian Gulf region—the location of the bulk of the world's low-cost oil reserves—to fulfill its vital requirements. Growing dependence on Persian Gulf suppliers has significant implications for the economic, diplomatic, and security interests of many nations, and especially those of the United States.

The world still obtains nearly half of all its energy from oil, and this finite source accounts for more than forty percent of the energy used by the United States. Thus it is understandable that oil is the most important component in the global energy outlook. Oil prices and oil supplies, both as they now stand and as they may develop, are clearly related to the way people both use and plan to use any source of energy.

As stated earlier, a buyer's market emerged throughout the 1980s for oil and other energy resources—the result of substantial price decreases for oil and competing fuels since their peak in 1981. Oil consumption in industrialized nations fell even while their economies expanded. In 1986, consumers reaped more advantages from this market shift as oil prices plummeted from about twenty-five dollars per barrel to about ten dollars per barrel, before rising in 1987 to slightly more than seventeen dollars per barrel.

Inflation, as a direct result of this price decrease, was lower than expected (in the United States inflation reached the lowest point in twenty-five years), leading to reduced interest rates worldwide. Such developments were welcomed by those less developed countries which were oil importers and already heavily in debt; in all of these countries, businesses and other consumers were able to use more oil at lower prices. As they spend and invest the resulting profits from such savings, the world economy should expand further and provide more jobs and higher incomes. On the other hand, petroleum is a depletable resource with a record of price volatility; therefore, a return to higher fuel costs at some point in the future is most likely.

More importantly, however, not everyone benefited from declining oil prices. In particular, oil producers in the United States and other nations saw their revenues and profits reduced sharply. Energy industries responded with a drastic economic retrenchment—laying off thousands of skilled workers and cutting back on the exploration and development of new oil reserves. Various other businesses, including firms that construct drilling rigs and other related oil field service companies, as well as many banks and industries, encountered severe financial difficulties. The debt problems of Mexico, Nigeria, Venezuela, and other oil-producing countries loomed even larger than before.

The current world energy situation and the outlook for the future include both opportunities and risks. The oil price decline of 1986 illustrated how consumers can benefit from a more competitive world oil market. If adequate supplies of oil and other energy resources continue to be available at reasonable prices, it will provide a boost to the world's economy. On the other hand, the projected increase in reliance on relatively few oil suppliers implies certain risks for the United States and the Western world. These risks can be summarized as: 1) if a small group of leading oil producers can dominate the world's energy markets, the result could be artifically high oil prices, or a combination of sharp upward and downward price swings. Both would necessitate difficult economic adjustments and cause hardship for consumers; 2) revolutions, regional conflicts, or military aggression from both internal and external powers could disrupt oil supplies from the Persian Gulf and inflict severe damage on the world economy. Oil price increases precipitated by the 1978-79 Iranian Revolution contributed to the world's largest economic recession since the 1930s. Also, the 1990 Iraqi invasion of Kuwait sent world oil prices soaring, worsening inflation and cutting into the purchasing power of the world's inhabitants. Worried consumers in the United States and elsewhere abruptly reduced spending, starting a recession that was still being felt in the summer of 1991. Similar events in the future would obviously have far-reaching economic, geopolitical, and possibly even military repercussions.

Yet the energy situation might well be viewed differently, because both the U.S. and the rest of the world are endowed with large reserves of energy resources. Oil is concentrated in the Middle East, in the less developed countries located mainly along the equatorial belt, and in the Soviet Union. Natural gas is similarly distributed, but with the largest share concentrated in the USSR, not in the Persian Gulf. Coal reserves overwhelm those of oil and natural gas, with the largest share in the United States; indeed, these reserves could satisfy America's current level of energy consumption well into the twenty-third century.

In addition to such "proven" resources, significant discoveries of other reserves are likely to occur. Even larger hydrocarbon deposits of tar sands, heavy oil, shale oil, and other forms would likely become more available were oil prices to rise. Combined with nuclear power and solar and geothermal energy, the world's energy resources, in theory, could support even the most rapid increases in global energy demand for many years to come. Access to these untapped or underdeveloped resources, however, may be constrained by a number of economic, geopolitical, and environmental factors.

In 1988 (the latest year for which complete data are available), the United States drew its energy supplies from an array of sources. Oil provided the largest single share of energy consumed, accounting for about forty-three percent of the total. Of this, well over half was produced domestically. Net imports of oil and oil-based products amounted to about 6.6 million barrels per day, the highest level since 1977.

Coal and natural gas made virtually identical contributions toward meeting America's demand for energy, each accounting for an additional twenty-three percent of the nation's total energy. Ninety-three percent of the natural gas and virtually one hundred percent of the coal used were produced domestically. Nuclear power and hydroelectric power added seven percent and three percent, respectively, with other forms of energy making up the remaining balance of less than one percent.

In 1988 OPEC produced one-third of all oil consumed in the world, then about twenty-two million barrels per day. Depending upon the increase in oil demand, OPEC production could range between twenty-eight million and forty million barrels per day by the year 2010. The most likely range for world oil prices in the year 2000 is twenty-to-thirty-four dollars per barrel, compared with eighteen dollars per barrel in 1989. By 2010 the range is likely to be twenty-six-to-forty-six dollars per barrel. (All prices are in constant U.S. dollars.)

OPEC accounts for nearly three of every four barrels of the world's total oil reserves, estimated in excess of 900 billion barrels. Increased production will not occur uniformly among all OPEC members, however, but will come primarily from an "inner core" of five Persian Gulf states that each have vast, low-cost oil resources: Saudi Arabia, Kuwait, Iraq, Iran, and the United Arab Emirates. Five countries—China, Mexico, Norway, the United States, and the Soviet Union—hold the majority of non-OPEC oil reserves.

By 2010 oil consumption in the market economies should continue to grow from the 1990s' approximately fifty-three million barrels per day to perhaps as much as sixty-five million barrels per day. Most of the increase in oil consumption among the industrialized nations that belong to the Organization for Economic Cooperation and Development (OECD) is expected to occur in the United States. The U.S., the major producer of oil among the OECD members, will supplement domestic production by importing more oil.

Among market economies in the less developed countries, additional growth in oil consumption is expected. Within the LDCs, such growth in oil consumption among OPEC nations will be limited by demand factors, primarily by the completion of petrochemical projects that use oil inputs. Oil consumption and production among the remaining LDCs were estimated to be just under eleven million barrels per day in 1990. However, while oil production is projected to peak at this general level, oil consumption should continue to grow at about one percent through the year 2010. Among the centrally planned economies, oil consumption will fall proportionally as reserves decline.

Several reasons exist for the relatively rapid growth in energy consumption among the LDCs. "Non-commercial" energy resources such as firewood, excluded from this discussion, are rapidly being replaced by "commercial" energy sources, such as electricity and kerosene, due to both rising incomes and increasing urbanization. The amount of energy-using equipment, such as refrigerators, motor scooters, and automobiles, while low in many developing countries, is rising quickly in LDCs. India, Brazil, Mexico, South Korea, Singapore, Taiwan, and China are all rapidly developing energy-intensive basic industries, such as steel mills and petrochemical plants. These basic industries produce the inputs to supply growing markets for energy-consuming equipment.

It is also necessary to recognize that energy demand should increase more slowly among the OECD countries than among the LDCs. The OECD nations are most capable, technically and financially, of implementing energy efficient measures. The accumulation of energy-based equipment, such as refrigerators and automobiles, in OECD nations is much nearer to the saturation point. Resultingly, future increases in consumption may be more responsive to household formation and population growth than to general economic development.

Oil will continue to be the world's single most important source of energy for the next twenty years, but its relative importance will continue to decline, from thirty-nine percent of the total energy used in 1988 to about thirty-two percent of the total used in 2010. The importance of all other major fuels, such as coal, for example, is expected to increase proportionally.

Against this backdrop, 1989 could have been much like 1988, when OPEC production rose sharply and prices were at their lowest levels since the 1986 oil price collapse. However, oil prices throughout the world rose, unadjusted for inflation, by more than three dollars per barrel in 1989. This rise, following a three and one-half dollar decrease per barrel in 1988, surprised many observers because it occurred despite an increase in OPEC production of 1.4 million barrels per day. Several factors enabled OPEC to increase its market share without causing world oil prices to drop. The primary reason was stronger-than-anticipated demand for oil products by the market economies. Demand increased by 1.2 million barrels per day, equivalent to 2.4 percent, from 1988's rate.

Long-Term Trends

Beyond the mid-1990s, the forecast is for oil prices to rise, for non-OPEC production to peak and then level off, and for oil production in the United States to continue to decline. Many analysts were surprised at the strong level of the demand for oil from 1988 to 1990, and many believe that such demand is a lingering re-

125

sponse to the low prices that have prevailed since the oil price collapse of 1986. Demand in the market economies is expected to continue increasing as a response to the relatively low oil prices anticipated throughout the world, prices which should remain low over the next several years. Even if oil prices should rise over the next few years, prices will still be relatively low when compared to their historically high levels of the early 1970s.

World oil prices have fluctuated during the past two decades, with price increases resulting in cutbacks in demand, and steadily declining prices encouraging more consumption and equivalent economic growth. Based on past experiences with price swings and the recent strong increases in demand, there is reason to believe that the relatively low prices forecast until the mid-1990s may result in demand increases that could lead to prices rising yet again.

The degree to which oil prices may rise depends largely upon OPEC's behavior. Future OPEC production decisions will be determined by a variety of factors. Market forces determine the overall limits within which OPEC can influence world oil markets, but, within these limits, market share and revenue goals, as well as political and security considerations, will exert great influence on how much oil OPEC decides to produce. The most likely course is that pressure to earn more revenue, along with the expected increase in demand for OPEC oil, will continue to encourage OPEC members to increase their production. However, uncertainties will remain concerning both the demand for oil and the terms on which it will be supplied by OPEC and non-OPEC nations. Oil supply, demand, and price will depend on the rate of recovery from the current world recession, the growth of the world economy, and the pace of energy substitution for oil.

In the event of yet another Arab-Israeli war, an Iraqi-Iranian military confrontation, or the attempt by one Gulf state to annex another, the world should expect the disruption of Middle Eastern oil deliveries and a consequent hike in prices. Under normal circumstances, OPEC members can no longer afford to raise prices indiscriminately because such actions will hurt their allies and friends in the Third World more than it will the West. Nonetheless, oil prices will remain subject to some manipulation by OPEC. After all, oil is OPEC's major political weapon and, although prices may neither rise nor drop significantly, consumers should be ever mindful that fortunate and fortuitous are not synonymous terms in OPEC's vocabulary.

ACRONYMS

AEC	Atomic Energy Commission
BENELUX	Belgium, The Netherlands, Luxembourg
CIA	Central Intelligence Agency
COMECON/CMEA	Council of Mutual Economic Assistance
ECAL	Economic Council of the Arab League
ERDA	Energy Research & Development Administration
EEC	European Economic Community
IEA	International Energy Agency
IMF	International Monetary Fund
LDCs	Less Developed Countries
MSAs	Most Severely Affected Countries
NPC	National Petroleum Council
NATO	North Atlantic Treaty Organization
NRC	Nuclear Regulatory Commission
OAPEC	Organization of Arab Petroleum Exporting Countries
OECD	Organization for Economic Cooperation and Development
OPEC	Organization of Petroleum Exporting Countries
PEN	Petroleum Exporting Nations
PLO	Palestine Liberation Organization
TAPLINE	Trans-Arabian Pipeline
UAE	United Arab Emirates
UN	United Nations
UNESCO	U.N. Educational, Scientific, and Cultural Organization

APPENDIX A

The Statute of the Organization of Petroleum Exporting Countries

Chapter I

Organization and Objectives

Article 1

The Organization of Petroleum Exporting Countries (OPEC), hereunder referred to as "the Organization," created as a permanent intergovernmental organization in conformity with the resolutions of the conference of the representatives of the governments of Iran, Iraq, Kuwait, Saudi Arabia, and Venezuela, held in Baghdad from September 10-14, 1960, shall carry out its functions in accordance with the provisions set forth hereunder.

Article 2

A. The principal aim of the Organization shall be the coordination and unification of the petroleum policies of member countries and the determination of the means of safeguarding their interests, individually and collectively.

B. The Organization shall devise ways and means of ensuring the stabilization of prices in international oil markets with a view to eliminating harmful and unnecessary fluctuations.

C. Due regard shall be given at all times to the interests of the producing nations and to the necessity of securing a steady income to the producing countries; an efficient, economic, and regular supply of petroleum to consuming nations; and a fair return on their capital to those investing in the petroleum industry.

Article 3

The Organization shall be guided by the principle of the sovereign equality of its member countries. Member countries shall fulfill, in good faith, the obligations assumed by them in accordance with the statute.

Article 4

If, as a result of the application of any decision of the Organization, sanctions are employed, directly or indirectly, by any interested company or companies against one or more member countries, no other member shall accept any offer of a beneficial treatment, whether in the form of an increase in oil exports or in an improvement in prices, which may be made to it by such interested company or companies with the intention of discouraging the application of the decision of the Organization.

Article 5

The Organization shall have its headquarters at the place the conference decides upon.

Article 6

English shall be the official language of the Organization.

Chapter II

Membership

Article 7

A. Founder members of the Organization are those countries which were represented at the first conference, held in Baghdad, and which signed the original agreement of the establishment of the Organization.

B. Full members shall be the founder members as well as those countries whose application for membership has been accepted by the conference.

C. Any other country with a substantial net export of crude petroleum, which has fundamentally similar interests to those of member countries, may become a full member of the Organization, if accepted by a majority of three-fourths of full members, including the concurrent vote of all founder members.

D. A net petroleum-exporting country which does not qualify for membership under paragraph C above may nevertheless be admitted as an associate member by the conference under such special conditions as may be prescribed by the conference, if accepted by a majority of three-fourths including the concurrent vote of all founder members.

No country may be admitted to associate membership which does not fundamentally have interests and aims similar to those of member countries.

E. Associate members may be invited by the conference to attend any meeting of a conference, the Board of Governors, or consultative meetings, and to participate in their deliberations without the right to vote. They are, however, fully entitled to benefit from all general facilities of the Secretariat including its publications and library as any full member.

F. Whenever the words "members" or "member countries" occur in this statute, they mean a full member of the Organization unless the context otherwise demonstrates to the contrary.

Article 8

A. No member of the organization may withdraw from membership without giving notice of its intention to do so to the conference. Such notice shall take effect at the beginning of the next calendar year after the date of its receipt by the conference, subject to the member having at that time fulfilled all financial obligations arising out of its membership.

B. In the event of any country having ceased to be a member of the Organization, its readmission to membership shall be made in accordance with Article 7, paragraph C.

Chapter III

Organs

Article 9

The Organization shall have three organs: I. The Conference; II. The Board of Governors; and III. The Secretariat.

I. The Conference

Article 10

The conference shall be the supreme authority of the Organization.

Article 11

A. The conference shall consist of delegations representing the member countries. A delegation may consist of one or more delegates, as well as advisers and observers. When a delegation consists of more than one person, the appointing country shall nominate one person as the head of the delegation.

B. Each member country should be represented at all conferences; however, a quorum of three-quarters of member countries shall be necessary for holding a conference.

C. Each full member country shall have one vote. All decisions of the conference, other than on procedural matters, shall require the unanimous agreement of all full members.

The conference resolutions shall become effective after 30 days from the conclusion of the meeting or after such period as the conference may decide unless, within the said period, the secretariat receives notification from member countries to the contrary.

In the case of a full member being absent from the meeting of the conference, the resolutions of the conference shall become effective unless the secretariat receives a notification to the contrary from the said member at least 10 days before the date fixed for publication of the resolutions.

D. A non-member country may be invited to attend a conference as an observer, if the conference so decides.

Article 12

The conference shall hold two ordinary meetings a year. However, an extraordinary meeting of the conference may be convened at the request of a member country by the secretary general, after consultation with the president and approval by a simple majority of the member countries. In the absence of unanimity among member countries approving the convening of such a meeting, as to the date and venue of the meeting, they shall be fixed by the secretary general in consultation with the president.

Article 13

The conference shall normally be held at the headquarters of the Organization, but it may meet in any of the member countries, or elsewhere as may be advisable.

Article 14

A. The conference shall elect a president and an alternate president at its first preliminary meeting. The alternate president shall exercise the responsibilities of the president during his absence or when he is unable to carry out his responsibilities.

B. The president shall hold office for the duration of the meeting of the conference, and shall retain the title until the next meeting.

C. The secretary general shall be the secretary of the conference.

Article 15

The conference shall:

1. formulate the general policy of the Organization and determine the appropriate ways and means of its implementation;
2. decide upon any application for membership of the Organization;
3. confirm the appointment of members of the Board of Governors;
4. direct the Board of Governors to submit reports or make recommendations on any matters of interest to the Organization;
5. consider, or decide upon, the reports and recommendations submitted by the Board of Governors on the affairs of the Organization;
6. consider and decide upon the budget of the Organization, as submitted by the Board of Governors;
7. consider and decide upon the statement of accounts and the auditor's report, as submitted by the Board of Governors;
8. call a consultative meeting for such member countries, for such purposes and in such places, when the conference deems fit;
9. approve any amendments to this statute;
10. appoint the chairman of the Board of Governors and an alternate chairman;
11. appoint the secretary general;
12. appoint the deputy secretary general; and
13. appoint the auditor of the Organization for a duration of one year.

Article 16

All matters that are not expressly assigned to other organs of the Organization shall fall within the competence of the conference.

II. The Board of Governors

Article 17

A. The Board of Governors shall be composed of governors nominated by the member countries and confirmed by the conference.

B. Each member of the Organization should be represented at all meetings of the Board of Governors; however, a quorum of two-thirds shall be necessary for the holding of a meeting.

C. When, for any reason, a governor is prevented from attending a meeting of the Board of Governors, a substitute ad hoc governor shall be nominated by the corresponding member country. Such nomination shall not require confirmation by the conference. At the meetings which he attends the ad hoc governor shall have the same status as the other governors, except as regards qualifications for chairmanship of the Board of Governors.

D. Each governor shall have one vote. A simple majority vote of attending governors shall be required for decision of the Board of Governors.

E. The term of office of each governor shall be two years.

Article 18

A. The Board of Governors shall meet no less than twice each year at suitable intervals to be determined by the chairman of the Board, after consultation with the secretary general.

B. An extraordinary meeting of the Board of Governors may be convened at the request of the chairman of the Board, the secretary general, or two-thirds of the governors.

Article 19

The meetings of the Board of Governors shall normally be held at the headquarters of the Organization, but they may also be held in any of the member countries, or elsewhere as may be advisable.

Article 20

The Board of Governors shall:

1. direct the management of the affairs of the Organization and the implementation of the decisions of the conference;
2. consider and decide upon any reports submitted by the secretary general;
3. submit reports and make recommendations to the conference on the affairs of the Organization;
4. draw up the budget of the Organization for each calendar year and submit it to the conference for approval;
5. nominate the auditor of the Organization for a duration of one year;
6. consider the statement of accounts and the auditor's report and submit them to the conference for approval;
7. approve the appointment of directors of divisions and heads of departments, upon nomination by the member countries, due consideration being given to the recommendations of the secretary general;
8. convene an extraordinary meeting of the conference;
9. nominate a deputy secretary general for appointment by the conference; and
10. prepare the agenda for the conference.

Article 21

The chairman of the Board of Governors and the alternate chairman, who shall assume all the responsibilities of the chairman whenever the chairman is absent or unable to exercise his responsibilities, shall be appointed by the conference from among the governors for a period of one year, in accordance with the principle of alphabetical rotation. The date of membership in the Organization, however, shall take precedence over the principle of alphabetical rotation.

Article 22

The chairman of the Board of Governors shall:

1. preside over the meetings of the Board of Governors;
2. attend the headquarters of the Organization in preparation for each meeting of the Board of Governors; and
3. represent the Board of Governors at conferences and consultative meetings.

Article 23

Should a majority of two-thirds of governors decide that the continuance of membership of any governor is detrimental to the interests of the Organization, the chairman of the Board of Governors shall immediately communicate this decision to the member country affected, who in turn shall nominate a substitute for the said governor before the next meeting of the Board of Governors. The nomination of such substitute as a governor shall be subject to confirmation by the following conference.

Article 24

Should a governor, for any reason, be precluded from continuing in the performance of his functions on the Board of Governors, the corresponding member country shall nominate a replacement. The nominated governor shall assume his functions upon nomination subject to confirmation by the following conference.

III. The Secretariat

Article 25

The secretariat shall carry out the executive functions of the Organization in accordance with the provisions of this statute under the direction of the Board of Governors.

Article 26

The secretariat of the Organization shall consist of the secretary general, the deputy secretary general, and such staff as may be required. It shall function at the headquarters of the Organization.

Article 27

A. The secretary general shall be the legally authorized representative of the Organization.

B. The secretary general shall be the chief officer of the secretariat, and in that capacity shall have the authority to direct the affairs of the Organization, in accordance with directions of the Board of Governors.

Article 28

A. The conference shall appoint the secretary general for a period of three years which term of office may be renewed once for the same period of time. This appointment shall take place upon nomination by member countries and after a comparative study of the nominees' qualifications.

The minimum personal requirements for the position of the secretary general shall be as follows:

a) 35 years of age.

b) A degree from a recognized university in Law, Economics, Science, Engineering, or Business Administration.

c) 15 years experience, of which at least 10 years should have been spent in positions directly related to the oil industry, and 5 years in highly responsible executive or managerial positions. Experience in government-company relations and in the international aspects of the oil industry is desirable.

Should in any case a unanimous decision not be obtained, the secretary general, in that case, shall be appointed on rotation basis for a term of two years without prejudice to the required qualifications.

B. The secretary general shall be a national of one of the member countries of the Organization.

C. The secretary general shall reside at the headquarters of the Organization.

D. The secretary general shall be responsible to the Board of Governors for all activities of the secretariat. The functions of the different departments shall be carried out on his behalf and under his authority and direction.

E. The secretary general shall attend all meetings of the Board of Governors.

Article 29

The secretary general shall:

1. organize and administer the work of the Organization;

2. ensure that the functions and duties assigned to the different departments of the secretariat are carried out;

3. prepare reports for submission to each meeting of the Board of Governors concerning matters which call for consideration and decision;

4. inform the chairman and other members of the Board of Governors of all activities of the secretariat, of all studies undertaken, and of the progress of the implementation of the resolutions of the conference; and

5. ensure the due performance of the duties which may be assigned to the secretariat by the conference or the Board of Governors.

Article 30

A. The deputy secretary general shall be selected by the Board of Governors from amongst the highly-qualified and experienced national candidates put forward by the member countries, for appointment by the conference by a vote of two-thirds of full members including the concurrent vote of at least three founder members.

B. The term of service of the deputy secretary general shall be for a period of three years. It may be extended for a period of one year or more, at the suggestion of the Board of Governors and with the approval of the conference.

C. The deputy secretary general shall reside permanently at the headquarters of the Organization.

D. The deputy secretary general shall be responsible to the secretary general for the coordination of the research and administrative activities of the secretariat. The functions of the different departments are exercised under the general supervision of the deputy secretary general.

E. The secretary general may delegate some of his authority to the deputy secretary general.

F. The deputy secretary general shall act for the secretary general, whenever the latter is absent from headquarters.

Article 31

A. The directors of divisions and heads of departments shall be appointed by the secretary general with the approval of the Board of Governors.

B. Officers of the secretariat, upon nomination by their respective governments, or by direct recruitment, shall be appointed by the secretary general in accordance with the staff regulations. In making such appointments, the secretary general shall give due consideration, as far as possible, to an equitable nationality distribution among members, but such consideration shall not be allowed to impair the efficiency of the secretariat.

Article 32

The staff of the secretariat are international employees with an exclusively international character. In the performance of their duties, they shall neither seek nor accept instructions from any government or from any other authority outside the Organization. They shall refrain from any action which might reflect on their position as international employees and they shall undertake to carry out their duties with the sole object of bearing the interests of the Organization in mind.

Article 33

1. The secretary general shall be assisted in the discharge of his duties by the deputy secretary general, a division of research, a personnel and administrative department, a public information department, a news agency, any division or department the conference may see fit to create, and his own office.

2. The OPEC News Agency (OPECNA) shall be a special unit responsible for collecting, producing, and disseminating news of general interest regarding the Organization and the member countries on energy and related matters.

3. The office of the secretary general shall provide him with executive assistance, particularly in carrying out contacts with governments, organizations, and delegations; in matters of protocol; in the preparation for and coordination of meetings; and other duties assigned by the secretary general.

4. Notwithstanding the provisions of Article 34, and where the efficient functioning of the divisions and departments of the secretariat so require, the Board of Governors may, upon the recommendation of the secretary general, authorize the secretary general to transfer functions of minor units from one division or department to another.

Article 34

A. The divison of research shall be responsible for:

1. conducting a continuous program for research, fulfilling the needs of the Organization, placing particular emphasis on energy and related matters;

2. monitoring, forecasting, and analyzing developments in the energy and petrochemical industries; and the evaluation of hydrocarbons and products and their non-energy uses;

3. analyzing economic and financial issues of significant interest, in particular those related to international financial and monetary matters, and to the international petroleum industry; and

4. maintaining and expanding data services to support the research activities of the secretariat and those of member countries.

B. The personnel and administration department shall:

1. be responsible for all organization methods, the provision of administrative services for all meetings, personnel matters, budgets, accounting, and internal control;

2. study and review general administrative policies and industrial relations methods used in the oil industry in member and other countries, and advise member countries of any possible improvements; and

3. keep abreast of the current administrative policies and/or policy changes occurring in the international petroleum industry which might affect the Organization or be of interest to it.

C. The public information department shall be responsible for:

1. presenting OPEC objectives, decisions, and actions in their true and most desirable perspective;

2. carrying out a central public information program and identifying suitable areas for the promotion of the Organization's aims; and

3. the production and distribution of publications and other materials.

Article 35

A. The secretary general shall commission consultants, as necessary, to advise on special matters or to conduct expert studies when such work cannot be undertaken by the secretariat.

B. The secretary general may engage such specialists or experts, regardless of nationality, as the Organization needs, for a period to be approved by the Board of Governors, provided there is a provision for such appointment in the budget.

C. The secretary general may at any time convene working parties to carry out any studies on specific subjects of interest to the member countries.

Chapter IV

Consultative Meetings and Specialized Organs

Article 36

A. A consultative meeting shall be composed of heads of delegations of member countries or their representatives.

B. In case a conference is not in session, a consultative meeting may be convened at any time at the request of the president of the conference.

C. The agenda of each consultative meeting shall be prepared by the president of the conference, unless it has been previously specified by the conference itself.

D. The consultative meeting may pass decisions or recommendations to be approved by the next conference unless otherwise authorized by a previous conference.

Article 37

A. The conference may establish specialized organs, as circumstances require, in order to assist in resolving certain problems of particular importance. The specialized organs shall function in accordance with the resolutions of statutes prepared to that effect.

B. The specialized organs shall operate within the general framework of the secretariat of the Organization, both functionally and financially.

C. The specialized organs shall act at all times in accordance with the principles of the Organization, as set out in the resolutions of the conference.

Chapter V

Financial Provisions

Article 38

A. The budget of the Organization shall be drawn up for each calendar year.

B. The conference, in accepting any associate member to the Organization, shall ask it to pay a fixed subscription to be considered as its financial contribution to the Organization.

C. Budget appropriations shall be apportioned on an equal basis among all member countries, after taking into consideration the annual subscriptions of the associate members.

Article 39

A. Each member country shall bear all expenses incurred in sending delegations or representatives to conferences, consultative meetings, and working parties.

B. The Organization shall bear the traveling expenses and remuneration of the governors who attend the meetings of the Board of Governors.

Chapter VI

Additional Provisions

Article 40

Amendments to this statute may be proposed by any member country. Such proposed amendments shall be considered by the Board of Governors which, if it so decides, shall recommend their adoption to the conference.

Article 41

All resolutions contrary to the context of this statute shall be abrogated.

Article 42

This statute shall be applied from May 1, 1965.

Source: *The Statute of the Organization of Petroleum Exporting Countries* (Vienna, Austria: Organization of Petroleum Exporting Countries, July 1980).

APPENDIX B

Resolution of Arab Oil Ministers

The oil ministers of the Organization of Arab Petroleum Exporting Countries (OAPEC) held a meeting in Kuwait on October 17, 1973 to consider the role of oil in the Arab people's current struggle to liberate their lands. Following through this question, the oil ministers,

Considering that the ultimate goal of the current struggle is the liberation of the Arab territories occupied by Israel in the 1967 War, and the restoration of the legitimate rights of the Palestinian people in accordance with United Nations resolutions,

Considering that the United States is the principal and foremost source of Israeli power that enables it to continue occupying their territories,

Considering that the industrial nations have a responsibility for implementing the United Nations resolutions, and

Considering that the economic situation of many Arab oil producing countries does not justify raising oil production, although they are willing to make an increase to meet the demand of those industrial nations that are committed to cooperation in the task of liberating occupied territories,

Decided that each Arab oil exporting country immediately cut its oil production by a rate not less than 5 percent from the September production level, and further increases of 5 percent from each of the following months, until such time as the international community compels Israel to relinquish occupied Arab lands, and to levels that will not undermine their economies or their national Arab obligations.

Countries supporting the Arab cause and those taking active and effective measures in compelling Israeli withdrawal shall not be affected by this production cut and shall continue to receive the same amount of oil supplies. The decrease in oil supply will be proportional to each outside country's degree of support and cooperation with the Israeli enemy.

The oil ministers also recommend that the United States should be subjected to the most severe cuts in the supply of crude oil and its refined products. This progressive reduction should lead to a total halt of oil supplies to the United States from each individual country participating in the meeting.

The Arab oil ministers met again in Kuwait on November 4, 1973, to discuss the question further and decided that the initial production cut be 25 percent of the September level, and a further 5 percent from the production of each of the following months. The 25 percent cut should also include the complete halt of all oil shipments to both the United States and the Netherlands.

The Arab Oil Halt to the United States and Holland

The Arab oil producing countries have decided to halt their oil supplies to the United States and Holland and to any other country supporting Israel.

This decision is by no means directed against the peoples of the United States or Holland. It is in fact directed against their governments' hostile policies toward the Arab people.

The Arab people fully realize the interests of other people and want to develop closer ties with the people of the United States and Holland, who must also realize where their interests lie.

The Arab Petroleum Exporting Countries would like the American and Dutch people to know that the halt in oil supplies to their countries will continue until such a time as Israeli forces are fully withdrawn from all occupied Arab territories and the Arab people of Palestine regain their lawful rights.

The Oil Ministers would like to draw the attention of the American people to the fact that the United States Government itself adopted similar policies of banning shipments of arms and strategic materiels, such as oil and food stuffs to countries considered hostile to the United States.

Source: *Resolution of the Arab Oil Ministers* (Washington, D.C.: Embassy of Kuwait, 1973).

NOTES

CHAPTER I

1. Tugendhat, Christopher, *Oil: The Biggest Business* (New York: G.P. Putnam's Sons, 1968), p. 71.
2. O'Connor, Harvey, *World Crisis in Oil* (New York: Monthly Review Press, 1962), p. 66.
3. *Op. cit.*, Tugendhat, p. 80.
4. *Ibid.*, p. 77-78.
5. *Ibid.*, p. 93.
6. Frankel, Paul H., *Essentials of Petroleum* (London: Chapman and Hall, 1940), p. 91.
7. Lufti, Ashraf, *OPEC Oil, Middle East Oil Monographs*, no. 6 (Beirut: Middle East Research and Publishing Center, 1968), p. 37.
8. *Op. cit.*, Tugendhat, p. 156.
9. *Ibid.*, p. 166-68.
10. *Ibid.*, p. 165.
11. Frank, Helmut J., *Crude Oil Price in the Middle East: A Study in Oligopolistic Behavior* (New York: Frederick A. Praeger, 1967), p. 10.
12. Hartshorn, J.E., *Politics of World Oil Economics* (New York: Frederick A. Praeger, 1967), p. 343.
13. Yager, Joseph A., and Eleanor B. Steinberg, *Energy and U.S. Foreign Policy* (Cambridge, Ma.: Ballinger Publishing Co., 1974), p. 14.
14. *Ibid.*
15. Miller, Roger LeRoy, *The Economics of Energy: What Went Wrong and How We Can Fix It* (New York: William Morrow and Co., 1974), p. 28-29.
16. Amuzegar, Jahangir, "The Oil Story: Fact, Fiction, and Fairplay," in *Foreign Affairs* (July, 1973): 682-683. It may be noted that within three months of the publication of this article, it became a fiction as OPEC unilaterally violated the most important clause of the Tehran Agreement on collective bargaining.
17. Crandall, Maureen S., "Oil in the Middle East and North Africa," in Erickson, Edward W. and Leonard Waverman, eds., *The Energy Question: An International Failure of Policy* vol. 1 (Toronto: University of Toronto Press, 1974), p. 65.
18. *Op. cit.*, Miller, p. 29.
19. Rifai, Taki, *The Pricing of Crude Oil: Economic and Strategic Guidelines for an International Energy Policy* (New York: Frederick A. Praeger, 1974), p. 263.
20. Petroleum Press Service, January 1973.
21. Jacoby, Neil H., *Multinational Oil: A Study in Industrial Dynamics* (New York: Macmillan Co., 1974), p. 259.
22. *Ibid.*, p. 260.
23. *Ibid.*
24. Insight Team of the *Sunday Times*, *Insight on the Middle East War* (London: Andre Deutsh, 1974), p. 178-79.
25. *The New York Times*, (Oct. 18, 1973).
26. *Op. cit.*, Insight Team.
27. *The New York Times Magazine*, (Mar. 24, 1974).
28. *Ibid.*
29. Magnus, Ralph H., "Middle East Oil," in *Current History* (February, 1975): 50.
30. Mikesell, Raymond F., et al., *Foreign Investments in the Petroleum and Mineral Industries* (Baltimore: Johns Hopkins University Press, 1971), p. 239.
31. Stauffer, Thomas R., "Oil Money and World Money: Conflict or Confluence?" in *Science* 184, no. 4134 (April 19, 1974): 332.
32. *Ibid.*
33. *Op. cit.*, Miller, p. 30.
34. *The Washington Post* (April 15, 1975).
35. *The New York Times*, (June 29 and July 4, 1979); and *Durham Morning Herald*, (Dec. 18, 1978).
36. Levy, Walter J., "Oil and the Decline of the West," in *Foreign Affairs* (Summer 1980): 1001; and *Congressional Quarterly: The Middle East* (Washington, D.C., Congressional Quarterly, 1981), p. 82.
37. *Petroleum Intelligence Weekly*, (July 20, 1981).
38. *Op. cit.*, Congressional Quarterly, p. 84.
39. Ismael, Tareq Y., *The Middle East in World Politics: A Study in Contemporary International*

Relations (Syracuse, NY: Syracuse University Press, 1974), p. 233.
40.   *Ibid.*
41.   *Ibid.*, p. 234.
42.   Laqueur, Walter, *Confrontation: The Middle East and World Politics* (New York: Bantam Books, 1974), p. 229.
43.   *The Middle East Economic Digest* (Dec. 7, 1973).

CHAPTER II

1.   Schurr, Sam H., and Paul T. Homan *et al.*, *Middle Eastern Oil and the Western World: Prospects and Problems* (New York: American Elsevier Publishing Co., 1971), p. 116.
2.   *Ibid.*, p. 117.
3.   Mikesell, Raymond F., *et al.*, *Foreign Investment in the Petroleum and Mineral Industries* (Baltimore: Johns Hopkins University Press, 1971), p. 225.
4.   Demares, Allan T., "Aramco is a Lesson in the Management of Chaos," in *Fortune* (Feb. 1974): 60-63.
5.   *Ibid.*, p. 63.
6.   *Newsweek* (July 1, 1974).
7.   Issawi, Charles, and Mohammaed Yeganeh, *The Economics of Middle Eastern Oil* (New York: Frederick A. Praeger, 1962), p. 47.
8.   Department of State, *Saudi Arabia: Background Notes* (Washington: U.S. Government Printing Office, May 1973), p. 3.
9.   Hartshorn, J. E., *Politics and World Oil Economics* (New York: Frederick A. Praeger, 1967), p. 56-57.
10.   Lenczowski, George, *Oil and State in the Middle East* (Ithaca, NY: Cornell University Press, 1960), p. 17.
11.   ____, ed., *United States Interests in the Middle East* (Washington, D.C.: American Enterprise Institute, 1968), p. 67.
12.   *The Washington Post, National Weekly Edition* (Oct. 22-28, 1990).
13.   Arabian American Oil Company, *Middle East Oil Development*, March 1956, p. 33.
14.   Mosley, Leonard, *Power Play: Oil in the Middle East* (Baltimore: Penguin Books, 1974), p. 424.
15.   United Nations, *Review of Economic Conditions in the Middle East*, E/1910 Add. 2/Rev.1 (New York: United Nations, 1951), p. 25.
16.   *Op. cit.*, Lenczowski, *Oil and State in the Middle East*, p. 19.
17.   *Saudi Arabian Monetary Agency, Annual Report, 1972*, (Jeddah: Research and Statistics Department, 1973), p. 20.
18.   *Op. cit.*, Mosley, p. 431-432. See this entry for a thorough account of the shares of various national and international oil companies operating in Saudi Arabia.
19.   *The Washington Post* (Feb. 5, 1974).
20.   *Ibid.*, Dec. 10, 1974.
21.   *Ibid.*, Dec. 14, 1974.
22.   *Ibid.*
23.   Monroe, Elizabeth, and Robert Mabro, *Oil Producers and Consumers: Conflict or Cooperation?* (New York: American Universities Field Staff, Inc., 1974), p. 17.
24.   *Ibid.*, p. 22.
25.   *The Oil and Gas Journal* (March 24, 1975).
26.   *Op. cit.*, Monroe and Mabro, p. 10.
27.   Sayegh, Kamal, *Oil and Arab Regional Development* (New York: Frederick A. Praeger, 1968), p. 297-298.
28.   *Op.cit.*, Lufti, p. 9.
29.   *Ibid.*, p. 10.
30.   Adelman, Morris A., *The World Petroleum Market* (Baltimore: Johns Hopkins University Press, 1972), p. 7.
31.   *Op. cit.*, Laqueur, p. 226.
32.   *Op. cit.*, Lufti, p. 37.

CHAPTER III

1.   *Op. cit.*, Lenczowski, *Oil and State in the Middle East*, p. 188.
2.   *Ibid.*
3.   *Ibid.*
4.   *Op. cit.*, Mosley, p. 343.
5.   *Ibid.*
6.   *Ibid.*, p. 344.
7.   *The Middle East Economic Survey* (Aug. 11, 1972).
8.   *Ibid.* (July 21, 1967).
9.   *Ibid.*
10.   *U.S. News & World Report* (Jan. 15, 1973).
11.   Kerr, Malcolm H., *The Arab Cold War* (London: Oxford University Press, 1971), p. 129.
12.   Safran, Nadav, "The War and the Future of the Arab-Israeli Conflict," in *Foreign Affairs* (January, 1974): 219.

13. See an English review of the original study in Arabic in *The Journal of Palestine Studies* (Autumn, 1973): 142-144.
14. *The Washington Post* (June 17, 1973).
15. *The Christian Science Monitor* (Sept. 4, 1973).
16. For the full text of the Arab oil ministers' resolution, see Appendix B.
17. *Ibid.*, p. 423.
18. *Op. cit.*, Safran, p. 220.
19. *Ibid.*, p. 221.
20. Schmidt, Dana Adams, *Armageddon in the Middle East* (New York: John Day Co., 1974), p. 212.
21. *Ibid.*
22. *The Economist*, (Nov. 3, 1973).
23. *The Daily Telegraph*, (Nov. 17, 1973).
24. *The Sunday Times* (Nov. 14, 1973).
25. *Op. cit.*, Schmidt, p. 213.
26. Lichtblau, John H., "Arab Oil and a Settlement of the Middle East Conflict," in *After the Settlement: New Directions and New Relationships* (Paper delivered at the 28th Annual Conference of the Middle East Institute, Washington, D.C., October 12, 1974).
27. *Ibid.*
28. *Ibid.*
29. *The Washington Post* (Dec. 24, 1973).
30. *Op. cit.*, Lichtblau.
31. *Ibid.*
32. Adapted from Joseph Kraft, "The Rising Price of Oil," in *The Washington Post* (Dec. 1, 1974).
33. *The Washington Post* (Dec. 31, 1973); and *The New York Times* (Dec. 31, 1973).
34. *Ibid.*
35. *Ibid.*
36. *The Washington Post* (Dec. 31, 1973).
37. *Ibid.*, (Dec. 26, 1973).
38. *The New York Times* (Oct. 18, 1973).
39. *The Middle East Economic Digest* (Mar. 22, 1974).
40. *The Washington Post* (Mar. 28, 1974).
41. *Op. cit.*, Lichtblau.
42. *Newsweek* (Mar. 25, 1974).
43. *Ibid.*
44. *The Arab Oil and Gas Journal* (May 1, 1974).
45. *Ibid.*
46. *Op.cit.*, Schmidt, p. 216.
47. *The Washington Post* (April 2, 1974).
48. Taylor, Alan R., "The Isolation of Israel," in *The Journal of Palestine Studies* (Autumn 1974): 93.
49. *The Middle East Economic Digest* (Mar. 22, 1974).
50. *Op. cit.*, Mosley, p. 426.
51. *Newsweek* (Mar. 25, 1974).
52. *The Middle East Economic Digest* (Dec. 28, 1973).
53. Al-Bazzaz, Mahdi, "Middle East Oil Revenues: An Assessment of Their Size and Uses," in *The Middle East Economic Digest* (Mar. 15, 1974).
54. *The New York Times* (Nov. 16, 1974).
55. *The Washington Post* (Nov. 23, 1974).
56. United Nations General Assembly Provisional Verbatim Record no. A/PV.2296, Nov. 22, 1974 (New York: United Nations), p. 46.
57. *The Washington Post* (Jan. 12, 1975).

CHAPTER IV

1. Said, Abdul A., ed., *America's World Role in the 70s* (Englewood Cliffs, NJ: Prentice Hall, 1970), p. 11.
2. Koenig, Louis W., ed., *The Truman Administrations: Its Principles and Practices* (Washington Square: New York University Press, 1956), p. 299.
3. Safran, Nadav, "Engagement in the Middle East," in *Foreign Affairs* (Oct. 1974): 49-50.
4. Rostow, Eugene V., "A Basis for Peace," in *The New Republic* (April 5, 1975): 12-13.
5. *Op. cit.*, Safran, p. 54.
6. *Ibid.*, p. 56.
7. Ball, George W., "The Looming War in the Middle East and How to Avert It," in *The Atlantic* (Jan. 1975): 10-11.
8. *Ibid.*, p. 6.
9. *The Washington Post* (Dec. 22, 1974).
10. *Ibid.*, (Mar. 28, 1975).
11. Congressional Quarterly, "The Middle East: U.S. Policy, Israel, Oil, and the Arabs" (Washington, D.C.: Congressional Quarterly, 1979), p. 35.
12. *The New York Times* (Mar. 17, 1977).

13.　See Congressional Quarterly, "The Middle East: U.S. Policy, Israel, Oil, and the Arabs" for a complete text of the joint statement.
14.　*Ibid.*, p. 4.
15.　*Ibid.*

CHAPTER V

1.　El Mallakh, Ragaei, "Oil and the OPEC Members," in *Current History* (July-August 1975): 6.
2.　Any nation can become a member of OPEC if it is a substantial net exporter of oil and is unanimously accepted by all five founding members—Iraq, Iran, Saudi Arabia, Kuwait, and Venezuela. The OPEC candidate should also have fundamentally similar political-economic interests with other members and be accepted by three-quarters of the full membership.
3.　*The Economist* (April 3, 1982).
4.　*The Wall Street Journal* (Dec. 15, 1980).
5.　Congressional Quarterly, "The Middle East" (Washington, D.C.: Congressional Quarterly, 1981), p. 82-83.
6.　Padelford, Norman J., *et al.*, *The Dynamics of International Politics* (New York: Macmillan Publishing, 1976), p. 382-383.
7.　Levy, Walter J., "Oil and the Decline of the West," in *Foreign Affairs*, (Summer 1980): 1001-1002.
8.　Ismael, Tareq Y., *The Middle East in World Politics: A Study in Contemporary International Relations* (Syracuse, NY: Syracuse University Press, 1974), p. 239.
9.　*The Durham Morning Herald* (Sept. 24, 1981).
10.　*The New York Times* (July 4, 1979).
11.　*Ibid.*
12.　*Bangladesh*, vol. 5, no. 18 (Oct. 1, 1975).
13.　From a speech by President Ziaur Rahman of Bangladesh at the 11th Special Session of the United Nations General Assembly in New York, August 26, 1980.
14.　*The New York Times* (Aug. 27, 1979).
15.　*Annual Report*, the International Monetary Fund, Washington, D.C., 1979.
16.　*The New York Times* (July 4, 1979).
17.　*The Durham Morning Herald* (Oct. 6, 1979).
18.　Askari, Hossein, and John Thomas Cummings, *Oil, OECD, and the Third World: A Vicious Triangle* (Austin, TX: Center for Middle Eastern Studies, University of Texas at Austin, 1978), p.37.
19.　*The Washington Post* (Aug. 27, 1979).
20.　Levy, Walter J., "The Years That the Locust Hath Eaten: Oil Policy and OPEC Development Prospects" in *Foreign Affairs*, (Winter 1978-79): 302.
21.　Annual Reports of the World Bank, 1975-79, Washington, D.C.
22.　Petroleum Intelligence Weekly (July 20, 1981).
23.　Levy, Walter J., "Oil and the Decline of the West," in *Foreign Affairs* (Summer 1980): 999.
24.　____, "Oil: An Agenda for the 1980s," in *Foreign Affairs* (Summer 1981): 1080.

CHAPTER VI

1.　Terrill, Ross, "China in the 1980s," in *Foreign Affairs* (Spring 1980): 931.
2.　Park, Choon-ho, and Jerome Alan Cohen, "The Politics of China's Oil Weapon," in *Foreign Policy* (Fall 1975): 29.
3.　*Ibid.*, p. 33.
4.　Saudi Arabia, United States, Soviet Union, Iran, Venezuela, Kuwait, Libya, Nigeria, Canada, Iraq, Indonesia, Algeria, and United Arab Republic.
5.　Harrison, Selig S., *China, Oil and Asia: Conflict Ahead* (New York: Columbia University Press, 1977), p. 19-20.
6.　*Far Eastern Economic Review* (Oct. 6, 1978).
7.　*Op. cit.*, Park and Cohen, p. 31.
8.　Cheng, Chu-yuan, "China's Energy Resources," in *Current History* (Sept. 1976): 74.
9.　Harrison, Selig S., "China: the Next Oil Giant," in *Foreign Policy* (Fall 1976): 6.
10.　Japan, North and South Korea, Taiwan, Malaysia, Vietnam, Indonesia, and the Philippines.
11.　*Newsweek* (Dec. 15, 1980).
12.　*Op. cit.*, Harrison. See chapters 4, 5, 6, 8, and 9 for an elaborate discussion of these claims and other ecopolitical issues relating to China's offshore oil claims.
13.　*Ibid.*, p. 252.
14.　*Newsweek* (Sept. 22, 1980).
15.　*Fortune* (Sept. 22, 1980).

CHAPTER VII

1.　Neal, Fred Warner, *Detente or Debacle: Common Sense in U.S. Soviet Relations* (New York: W.W. Norton and Co., 1979), p. 9.
2.　For details see Gillette, Phillip S., "American Capital in the Contest for Soviet Oil, 1920-

1923," in *Soviet Studies* XXIV, no. 4 (April 1972): 477-490.

3. Hartshorn, J.E., *Politics and World Oil Economics* (New York: Frederick A. Praeger, 1967), p. 235.
4. Campbell, Robert W., *The Economics of Soviet Oil and Gas* (Baltimore: Johns Hopkins University Press, 1967), p. 2, 121.
5. Payton-Smith, D.J., *Oil: A Study of War-Time Policy and Administration* (London: Her Majesty's Stationery Office, 1971).
6. Klinghoffer, Arthur Jay, *The Soviet Union and International Oil Politics* (New York: Columbia University Press, 1977), p. 182.
7. *Ibid.*
8. Dewar, Margaret, *Soviet Trade with Eastern Europe: 1945-1949* (London: Royal Institute of International Affairs, 1951), p. 78-79; and Jordan, Constantin, *The Romanian Oil Industry* (New York: New York University Press, 1955), p. 42 and 284-291.
9. *Op. cit.,* Campbell, p. 248.
10. Erickson Edward W., and Leonard Waverman, eds. *The Energy Question: An International Failure of Policy,* vol. 1 (Toronto: University of Toronto Press, 1974), p. 94-95.
11. *Ibid.,* p. 95.
12. *Op. cit.,* Klinghoffer, p. 28.
13. *Ibid.,* p. 267.
14. *Ibid.*
15. Farnsworth, Clyde, "U.S.-Soviet Grain Accord Nearly Failed," in *The New York Times* (Oct. 25, 1975).
16. Berry, John A., "Oil and Soviet Policy in the Middle East," in *The Middle East Journal* (Spring 1972): 150.
17. Longrigg, Stephen, *Oil in the Middle East* (London: Oxford University Press, 1968), p. 346.
18. Perlo, Victor, "American Oil Companies and the Middle East," in *International Affairs* no. 12, (Moscow, Dec. 1967): 44.
19. *Ibid.,* p. 40.
20. *Op. cit.,* Klinghoffer, p. 119.

CHAPTER VIII

1. Fisher, Sydney N., *The Middle East* (New York: Alfred A. Knopf, 1959), p. 583.
2. *Newsweek* (April 9, 1973).
3. *Newsweek* (Dec. 30, 1974).
4. Ullman, Richard H., "After Rabat: Middle East Risks and American Roles," in *Foreign Affairs* (January 1975): 287-288.
5. *Ibid.,* p. 289-290.
6. *Strategic Survey, 1973,* International Institute for Strategic Studies, London, 1974, p. 1.
7. *The Washington Post* (Nov. 16, 1974).
8. *The New York Times* (Sept. 24, 1974).
9. *Newsweek* (Dec. 23, 1974).
10. *Press Release no. Press/A (74) 48,* Nov. 15, 1974, Organization for Economic Cooperation and Development; and *The Washington Post,* (Nov. 16, 1974).
11. *Time* (Nov. 25, 1974).
12. *Business Week* (Jan. 13, 1975).

CHAPTER IX

1. *The New York Times* (Nov. 27, 1973).
2. *The Washington Post* (April 19, 1975).
3. Laird, Melvin R., "Let's Meet the Energy Crunch Now," in *Reader's Digest* (Jan. 1975): 50.
4. Wilson, Carroll L., "A Plan for Energy Independence," in *Foreign Affairs* (July 1973): 675.
5. MIT Energy Laboratory Policy Study Group, *Energy Self-Sufficiency: An Economic Evaluation,* (Washington: American Enterprise Institute for Public Policy Research, 1974), p. 69-70.
6. The *Durham Morning Herald* (April 27, 1982).
7. See *The Washington Post* (Jan. 12, 1975) for a complete report of the press conference by Senator Frank Church, Chairman of the Senate Foreign Relations Subcommittee on Multinational Corporations.
8. Energy Policy Project of the Ford Foundation, *A Time to Choose: America's Energy Future* (Cambridge, Ma.: Ballinger Publishing Co., 1974), p. 45-79.
9. *Ibid.,* p. 81-111.
10. *The Washington Star-News* (Dec. 18, 1974).
11. *Op. cit.,* Laird.
12. Rose, David J., "Energy Policy in the U.S.," in *Scientific American* 230, no. 1 (January 1974): 359.
13. *Ibid.*
14. National Petroleum Council, *U.S. Energy Outlook: An Interim Report* (Washington, D.C.: National Petroleum Council, 1972), p. 20; and *Newsweek* (Dec. 10, 1973).
15. Ramey, James T., "The Promise of Nuclear Energy," in *The Annals* (Nov. 1973): 23.
16. *Newsweek* (Nov. 12, 1973).

17. *Ibid.*
18. Clark, Wilson, *Energy for Survival: The Alternative to Extinction* (Garden City, NY: Anchor Books, 1974), p. 254.
19. *Op. cit.*, MIT Energy Laboratory Policy Study Group, p. 52-53.
20. *Op. cit.*, National Petroleum Council, p. 17, 44.
21. *Ibid.*, p. 37.
22. Rocks, Lawrence, and Richard P. Runyon, *The Energy Crisis* (New York: Crown Publishers, 1972), p. 40.
23. *Ibid.*, p. 39.
24. Ibid.
25. *Science* (June 15, 1973).
26. *The World Almanac 1974*, p. 115.
27. Hammond, Allen L., *et al.*, *Energy and the Future* (Washington, D.C.: American Association for the Advancement of Science, 1973), p. 12.
28. *Op. cit.*, Rocks and Runyon, p. 57.
29. *Op. cit.*, Hammond, p. 61.
30. *Op. cit.*, Clark, p. 370.
31. Lof, George O. G., "Solar Energy: An Infinite Source of Clean Energy," in *The Annals* (November 1973): 56.
32. *Op. cit.*, Energy Policy Project of the Ford Foundation, p. 51.
33. *Op. cit.*, Hammond, p. 60.
34. *Op. cit.*, Energy Policy Project of the Ford Foundation, p. 52.
35. *Op. cit.*, Hammond, p. 62-63.
36. *Op. cit.*, Lof, p. 52.
37. Wolf, Martin, "Solar Energy Utilization by Physical Methods," in *Science* 184, no. 4134 (April 1974): 386.

BIBLIOGRAPHY

Abir, Mordechai. *Oil, Power, and Politics: Conflict in Arabia, the Red Sea, and the Gulf*. London: Frank Cass, 1974.

Abolfathi, Farid, *et al. The OPEC Market to 1985*. Lexington, Ma.: Lexington Books, 1977.

Ali, Sheikh R. *Oil and Power: Politics Dynamics in the Middle East*. New York: St. Martin's Press, 1987.

____. *Oil, Turmoil, and Islam in the Middle East*. New York: Praeger, 1986.

____. *Saudi Arabia and Oil Diplomacy*. New York: Praeger, 1976.

Adelman, Morris A. *The World Petroleum Market*. Baltimore: Johns Hopkins University Press, 1972.

Arabian American Oil Company. *The Arabia of Ibn Saud*. New York: Arabian American Oil Company, 1952.

____. *Middle East Oil Development*. New York: Arabian American Oil Company, 1956.

____. *Oil and the Middle East*. Dhahran: Arabian American Oil Company, 1968.

Askari, Hossein, and John Thomas Cummings. *Oil, OECD, and the Third World: A Vicious Triangle*. Austin: Center for Middle Eastern Studies, University of Texas at Austin, 1978.

Assah, Ahmed. *Miracle of the Desert Kingdom*. London: Johnson Publishing Co., 1969.

Barrows, Gordon H. *The International Petroleum Industry*. New York: International Petroleum Institute, 1965.

Black, C.E. *The Dynamics of Modernization*. New York: Harper and Row, 1967.

Blair, John M. *The Control of Oil*. London: Macmillan, 1976.

Bohi, Douglas R. and Milton Russell. *Limiting Oil Imports*. Baltimore: Johns Hopkins University Press, 1978.

British Petroleum Company. *Statistical Review of the World Oil Industry*. London: British Petroleum Co., 1956.

Brooks, Michael. *Oil and Foreign Policy*. London: Lawrence and Wishart, 1949.

Brown, Seyom. *New Forces in World Politics*. Washington, D.C.: Brookings Institution, 1974.

Byroade, Henry A. *U.S. Foreign Policy in the Middle East*. Department of State Publication, no. 4852, Washington, D.C., 1953.

Caldwell, Malcolm. *Oil and Imperialism in East Asia*. Nottingham, England: Bertrand Russell Peace Foundation, 1971.

Caroe, Olaf. *Wells of Power: The Challenge to Islam: A Study in Contrast*. London: Macmillan, 1951.

Center for Study of the American Experience. *Energy in America: Fifteen Views*. Los Angeles: University of Southern California Press, 1980.

Chase Manhattan. *Capital Investments of the World Petroleum Industry*. New York: Chase Manhattan, 1976.

____. *The Profit Situation: A Special Petroleum Report*. New York: Chase Manhattan, 1974.

Chenery, Hollis, *et al. Redistribution With Growth*. London: Oxford University Press, 1974.

Cheney, Michael Sheldon. *Big Oilman from Arabia*. London: Heinemann, 1958.

Choucri, Nazli. *International Energy Future: Petroleum Prices, Power, and Payments*. Cambridge, Ma.: MIT Press, 1981.

Clark, Wilson. *Energy for Survival*. New York: Anchor Books, 1974.

Commoner, Barry. *The Closing Circle: Nature, Man, and Technology*. New York: Bantam Books, 1971.

Conant, Melvin. *Access to Energy: 2000 and After*. Lexington, Ky: University of Kentucky Press, 1979.

Congressional Quarterly. *Energy Crisis in America*. Washington, D.C.: Congressional Quarterly, 1973.

____. *The Middle East*. Washington, D.C.: Congressional Quarterly, 1981.

____. *The Middle East: U.S. Policy, Israel, Oil, and the Arabs*. Washington, D.C.: Congressional Quarterly, 1974 and 1979.

Darmstadter, Joel, *et al. Energy in the World Economy*. Baltimore: Johns Hopkins University Press, 1971.

Demir, Soliman. *Arab Development Funds in the Middle East*. Elmsford, NY: Pergamon Press, 1979.

Denny, Ludwell. *We Fight for Oil*. New York: Alfred A. Knopf, 1929.

Ebel, Robert E. *Communist Trade in Oil and Gas*. New York: Frederick A. Praeger, 1960.

Energy Policy Project of the Ford Foundation. *A Time to Choose: America's Energy Future*. Cambridge, Ma.: Ballinger Publishing Co., 1974.

Energy Systems Program Group of the International Institute for Applied Systems Analysis. *Energy in a Finite World: Paths to a Sustainable Future*. Cambridge, Ma.: Ballinger Publishing Co., 1981.

Engler, Robert. *The Politics of Oil*. New York: Macmillan, 1961.

Erickson, Edward W., and Leonard Waverman, eds. *The Energy Question: An International Failure of Policy, vol. 1*. Toronto: University of Toronto Press, 1974.

Evron, Yair. *The Middle East: Nations, Superpowers, and Wars*. New York: Frederick A. Praeger, 1973.

Exxon. *Middle East Oil*. New York: Exxon, 1976.

Falk, Richard A. *This Endangered Planet: Prospects and Proposals for Human Survival*. New York:

Vintage Books, 1971.

Fanning, Leonard M. *Foreign Oil and the Free World*. New York: McGraw Hill, 1954.

Finnie, David H. *Desert Enterprise: The Middle East Oil Industry in Its Local Environment*. Cambridge, Ma.: Harvard University Press, 1958.

Fischer, Louis. *Oil Imperialism: The International Struggle for Petroleum*. New York: International Publishers, 1926.

Fisher, Carol, and Fred Krinsky. *Middle East in Crisis*. Syracuse, NY: Syracuse University Press, 1959.

Fisher, John C. *Energy Crisis in Perspective*. New York: John Wiley and Sons, 1974.

Frank, Helmut J. *Crude Oil Prices in the Middle East: A Study in Oligopolistic Behavior*. New York: Frederick A. Praeger, 1967.

Frankel, P.H. *Essentials of Petroleum*. London: Chapman and Hall, 1940.

____. *Mattei: Oil and Power Politics*. New York: Frederick A. Praeger, 1966.

____. *Oil: The Facts of Life*. London: Weidenfeld and Nicolson, 1962.

Freeman, S. David. *Energy: The New Era*. New York: Vintage Books, 1974.

Gisselquist, David. *Oil Prices and Trade Deficits: U.S. Conflicts With Japan and West Germany*. New York: Frederick A. Praeger, 1979.

Hallwood, Paul and Stuart Sinclair. *Oil, Debt, and Development: OPEC in the Third World*. London: Allen and Unwin, 1981.

Hammond, Allen L., *et al. Energy and the Future*. Washington, D.C.: American Association for the Advancement of Science, 1973.

Hardy, Randall W. *China's Oil Future: A Case of Modest Expectations*. Boulder, Co: Westview Press, 1978.

Hartshorn, J.E. *Politics and World Oil Economics*. New York: Frederick A. Praeger, 1967.

Hill, P., and R. Vielvoye. *Energy in Crisis: A Guide to World Oil Supply and Demand and Alternative Resources*. London: Robert Yeatman, 1974.

____. *Energy in Crisis*. New York: Drake Publishers, 1975.

Hossain, Kamal. *Law and Policy in Petroleum Development*. New York: Nichols Publishing Co., 1979.

Houthakker, Hendrik S. *The World Price of Oil: A Medium Term Analysis*. Washington, D.C.: American Enterprise Institute for Public Policy Research, 1976.

Howell, Leon, and Michael Morrow. *Asia, Oil Politics and the Energy Crisis: The Haves and the Have-Nots*. New York: IDOC/North America, 1974.

Hurewitz, J.C., ed. *Oil, the Arab-Israel Dispute, and the Industrial World*. Boulder, Co: Westview Press, 1976.

Ickes, Harold L. *Fighting Oil*. New York: Alfred A. Knopf, 1943.

Inglis, K.A D., ed. *Energy: From Surplus to Scarcity?* New York: John Wiley and Sons, 1974.

Insight Team of the *Sunday Times. Insight on the Middle East War*. London: Andre Deutsch, 1974.

Ismail, Salem K. *The Correlation Between Energy Consumption and Gross National Product*. Vienna: Organization of Petroleum Exporting Countries, 1968.

Issawi, Charles, and Mohammed Yeganeh. *The Economics of Middle Eastern Oil*. New York: Frederick A. Praeger, 1962.

____. *Oil, the Middle East, and the Third World*. New York: The Library Press, 1972.

Jacoby, Neil H. *Multinational Oil: A Study in Industrial Dynamics*. New York: Macmillan Co., 1974.

Jensen, W.G. *Energy and the Economy of Nations*. Oxfordshire, England: G.T. Fouls and Co., 1970.

Johany, Ali D. *The Myth of the OPEC Cartel: The Role of Saudi Arabia*. New York: John Wiley and Sons, 1980.

Kennedy, William J., ed. *Secret History of the Oil Companies in the Middle East*. Salisbury, NC: Documentary Publications, 1980.

Kerr, Malcolm H. *The Arab Cold War: 1958-1970*. London: Oxford University Press, 1971.

Khera, S.S. *Oil Rich Man and Poor Man*. New Delhi: National Publishing House, 1979.

Khouri, Fred J. *The Arab-Israeli Dilemma*. Syracuse, NY: Syracuse University Press, 1968.

Klebanoff, Shoshana. *Middle East Oil and U.S. Foreign Policy*. New York: Frederick A. Praeger, 1974.

Klinghoffer, Arthur Jay. *The Soviet Union and International Oil Politics*. New York: Columbia University Press, 1977.

Landis, Lincoln. *Politics and Oil: Moscow in the Middle East*. New York: Dunellen Publishing Co., 1973.

Lenczowski, George. *The Middle East in World Affairs*. Ithaca, NY: Cornell University Press, 1962.

Longhurst, Henry. *Adventure in Oil: The Study of British Petroleum*. London: Sidgwick and Jackson, 1959.

Longrigg, Stephen H. *Oil in the Middle East: Its Discovery and Development*. London: Oxford University Press, 1961.

Lovins, Amory, *et al. The Energy Controversy: Soft Path Questions and Answers*. San Francisco: Friends of the Earth, 1979.

Lubell, Harold. *Middle East Oil Crisis and Western Europe's Energy Supply*. Baltimore: Johns Hopkins University Press, 1963.

Lufti, Ashraf. *Arab Oil: A Plan for the Future*. Beirut: Middle East Research and Publishing Center, 1960.

____. *OPEC Oil: Middle East Monographs*. no. 6. Beirut: Middle East Research and Publishing Center, 1968.

Macrakis, Michael S., ed. *Energy, Demand, Conservation, and Institutional Problems*. Cambridge, Ma.: MIT Press, 1974.

Makdisi, Samir A. *Middle East Problem Paper no. 12: Oil Price Increases and the World Economy*. Washington, D.C.: Middle East Institute, 1974.

Mancke, Richard. *The Failure of U.S. Energy Policy*. New York: Columbia University Press, 1974.

McCracken, Paul W. *Is the Energy Crisis Contrived?* Washington, D.C.: American Enterprise Institute for Public Policy Research, 1974.

McDonald, Stephen L. *Petroleum Conservation in the United States: An Economic Analysis*. Baltimore: Johns Hopkins University Press, 1971.

McLean, John G., and Robert W. Haigh. *The Growth of Integrated Oil Companies*. Boston: Harvard University Press, 1954.

Medvin, Norman. *The Energy Cartel: Who Runs the American Oil Industry?* New York: Vintage Books, 1974.

Mikdashi, Zuhayr M. *The Community of Oil Exporting Companies*. Ithaca, NY: Cornell University Press, 1972.

_____. *A Financial Analysis of Middle Eastern Oil Concessions: 1901-65*. New York: Frederick A. Praeger, 1966.

_____, and Hollis B. Chenery. *Arabian Oil*. Chapel Hill, NC: University of North Carolina Press, 1949.

Mikesell, Raymond F., *et al. Foreign Investment in the Petroleum and Mineral Industries*. Baltimore: Johns Hopkins University Press, 1971.

Miller, Aaron David. *Search for Security: Saudi Arabian Oil and American Foreign Policy*. Chapel Hill, NC: University of North Carolina Press, 1980.

Miller, Roger LeRoy. *The Economics of Energy: What Went Wrong and How We Can Fix It*. New York: William Morrow and Co., 1974.

MIT Energy Laboratory Policy Group. *Energy Self-Sufficiency: An Economic Evaluation*. Washington, D.C.: American Enterprise Institute for Public Policy Research, 1974.

Mitchell, Edward J., ed. *Dialogue on World Oil*. Washington, D.C.: American Enterprise Institute for Public Policy Research, 1974.

Mobley, Jonathan H. *The Elusive Peace: The Middle East, Oil, and the Economic and Political Future of the World*. Albuquerque, NM: Institute for Economic and Political World Strategic Studies, 1981.

Monroe, Elizabeth, and Robert Mabro. *Oil Producers and Consumers: Conflict or Cooperation*. New York: American Universities Field Studies, 1981.

Mosley, Leonard. *Power Play: Oil in the Middle East*. Baltimore: Penguin Books, 1974.

Mughraby, Muammad A. *Permanent Sovereignty Over Oil Resources*. Beirut: Middle East Research and Publishing Center, 1966.

Nash, Gerald D. *United States Oil Policy: 1890-1964*. Pittsburgh: University of Pittsburgh Press, 1968.

Nasrollah, S. Fatemi. *Oil Diplomacy: Powderkeg in Iran*. New York: Whittier Books, 1954.

National Petroleum Council. *Impact of New Technology on the U.S. Petroleum Industry: 1946-1965*. Washington, D.C.: National Petroleum Council, 1967.

_____. *U.S. Energy Outlook*. Washington, D.C.: National Petroleum Council, 1972.

Noreng, Oystein. *Oil Politics in the 1980s*. New York: McGraw-Hill, 1978.

O'Connor, Harvey. *World Crisis in Oil*. New York: Monthly Review Press, 1962.

O'Connor, Richard. *The Oil Barons: Men of Greed and Grandeur*. London: Hart-Davis/MacGibbon, 1972.

Odell, Peter R. *An Economic Geography of Oil*. New York: Frederick A. Praeger, 1963.

_____. *Oil and World Power: A Geographical Interpretation*. London: Cox and Wymen, 1972.

Odum, Howard T. *Environment, Power, and Society*. New York: John Wiley and Sons, 1971.

Pachachi, Nadim. *The Role of OPEC in the Emergence of New Patterns in Government-Company Relationships*. London: Royal Institute of International Affairs, 1972.

Penrose, Edith T. *The Growth of Firms, Middle East Oil, and Other Essays*. London: Frank Cass, 1971.

_____. *The Large International Firm in Developing Countries: The International Petroleum Industry*. London: George Allen and Unwin, 1968.

Prast, William G. *Securing U.S. Energy Supplies: The Private Sector as an Instrument of Public Policy*. Lexington, Ma.: Lexington Books, 1981.

Pringle, Laurence. *Energy: Power for People*. New York: Macmillan, 1975.

Rand, Christopher T. *Making Democracy Safe for Oil: Oilmen and the Islamic East*. Boston: Little, Brown, 1975.

Rifai, Taki. *The Pricing of Crude Oil: Economic and Strategic Guidelines for an International Energy Policy*. New York: Frederick A. Praeger, 1974.

Robertson, Nelson, ed. *Origins of the Saudi Arabian Oil Empire: Secret U.S. Documents, 1923-1944*. Salisbury, NC: Documentary Publications, 1980.

Rocks, Lawrence, and Richard P. Runyon. *The Energy Crisis*. New York: Crown Publishers, 1972.

Roosevelt, Kermit. *Arabs, Oil and History: The Story of the Middle East*. New York: Harper and Row, 1949.

Rouhani, Fuad. *A History of OPEC*. New York: Frederick A. Praeger, 1971.

Roumaini, Maurice M., ed. *Forces of Change in the Middle East*. Worcester, Ma.: Worcester State College Press, 1971.

Safer, Arnold. *International Oil Policy*. Lexington, Ma.: Lexington Books, 1979.

Safran, Nadav. *From War to War: The Arab-Israeli Confrontation, 1948-1967*. New York: Pegasus, 1969.

Said, Abdul A., and Luiz R. Simmons, eds. *The New Sovereigns: Multinational Corporations as World Powers*. Englewood Cliffs, NJ: Prentice-Hall, 1975.

144

Sayegh, Kamal S. *Oil and Arab Regional Development*. New York: Frederick A. Praeger, 1968.

Schurr, Sam H., *et al. Middle Eastern Oil and the Western World: Prospects and Problems*. New York: American Elsevier Publishing Co., 1971.

_____. *Energy in the American Economy 1850-1975: An Economic Study of its History and Prospects*. Baltimore: Johns Hopkins University Press, 1960.

Seymour, Ian. *OPEC: Instrument of Change*. New York: St. Martin's, 1981.

Schwadran, Benjamin. *The Middle East Oil and the Great Powers*. New York: Frederick A. Praeger, 1955.

Sinai, I. Robert, *et al. Modernization and the Middle East*. New York: American Academic Association for Peace in the Middle East, 1970.

Speigel, Steven L., ed. *At Issue: Politics in the World Arena*. New York: St. Martin's, 1973.

Stobaugh, Robert and Daniel Yergin. *Energy Future: Report of the Harvard Business School Energy Project*. New York: Random House, 1979.

Stocking, George W. *Middle East Oil: A Study in Political and Economic Controversy*. Kingsport, Tn.: Vanderbilt University Press, 1970.

Stork, Joe. *Middle East Oil and the Energy Crisis*. New York: Monthly Review Press, 1975.

Tahtinen, Dale R. *The Arab-Israeli Military Balance Today*. Washington, D.C.: American Enterprise Institute for Public Policy Research, 1973.

Tanzer, Michael. *Energy Crisis: World Struggle for Power and Wealth*. New York: Monthly Review Press, 1974.

_____. *The Political Economy of International Oil and the Underdeveloped Countries*. Boston: Beacon Press, 1969.

Tugendhat, Christopher. *Oil: The Biggest Business*. New York: G. P. Putnam's Sons, 1968.

Turner, Louis. *Oil Companies in the International System*. London: George Allen and Unwin, 1978.

Vicker, Ray. *The Kingdom of Oil*. New York: Charles Scribner's Sons, 1974.

Wilson, Rodney. *The Economics of the Middle East*. New York: Holmes and Meier, 1979.

Yager, Joseph A., and Eleanor B. Steinberg. *Energy and U.S. Foreign Policy*. Cambridge, Ma.: Ballinger Publishing Co., 1974.

Yannacone, Victor J., ed. *Energy Crisis: Danger and Opportunity*. St. Paul, Mn.: West Publishing Co., 1974.

INDEX

ABOUT THE AUTHORS

Dr. Sheikh R. Ali is a professor of political science at North Carolina Central University, at Durham. Professor Ali received his Ph.D. in International Studies in 1975 from American University in Washington, D.C., and master's degrees in government, political science, and international relations, and he was a Fulbright scholar at New York University. A former diplomat, Dr. Ali is an internationally known authority on petropolitics, and has published more than seventy-five books, articles, and reviews in a wide variety of American and international journals. His books in the field of world oil politics include *Saudi Arabia and Oil Diplomacy* (Praeger, 1976), *Oil, Turmoil, and Islam in the Middle East* (Praeger, 1986), and *Oil and Power: Political Dynamics in the Middle East* (St. Martin's Press, 1987). Dr. Ali presented a paper on the "Contemporary Islamic Resurgence in the Middle East" at the World Conference on Islam at Cornell University In 1988. A frequent traveler to the Middle East, in 1988 Dr. Ali served as part of the sixteen-member American Professors for Peace in the Middle East Study Mission in Israel and Egypt. In 1989 he was invited by the Persian Gulf Institute to attend an international conference on the Persian Gulf held in Tehran and to present a paper on "Persian Gulf Oil and World Energy Security." Dr. Ali is a member of many professional organizations, and in 1990 he was nominated for the O. Max Gardner Award, North Carolina's highest academic honor.

Dr. Jeffrey M. Elliot is a professor of political science at North Carolina Central University, at Durham. He received his Master of Arts in 1970 from the University of Southern California, and his Doctor of Arts from the Claremont Graduate School in 1978. In 1985, he was awarded an honorary Doctor of Humane Letters degree from Shaw University, and in 1986 The Jeffrey M. Elliot Collection, a permanent archive of his published works, was established at California State University, San Bernardino. A prodigious writer, he has authored sixty-two books and more than 500 articles, reviews, and interviews. His work has appeared in more than 250 publications, both in the United States and abroad, and has been nominated for nearly seventy literary awards. Also a free-lance journalist, Dr. Elliot has conducted more than 350 interviews with such figures as Jimmy Carter, Fidel Castro, and Yasir Arafat. Dr. Elliot also serves as Distinguished Advisor on Foreign Affairs to California Congressman Mervyn M. Dymally, and as editor or contributing editor to six journals. *The Work of Jeffrey M. Elliot: An Annotated Bibliography and Guide* was published by The Borgo Press in 1986, and in 1983 Borgo published Dr. Elliot's book *Tempest in a Teapot: The Falkland Islands War*.